YOU ARE A
THEOLOGIAN
THINKING **RIGHT** ABOUT **GOD**

BEN GISELBACH

To my dad;
a truly godly father,
whose character and example
during my formative years
made it natural for me
to love my heavenly Father
more than life itself.

"I will be a father to you,
and you shall be sons and daughters to me,
says the Lord Almighty"
(2 Corinthians 6:18)

"Besides this, we have had earthly fathers
who disciplined us and we respected them.
Shall we not much more be subject
to the Father of spirits and live?"
(Hebrews 12:9)

WITH MANY THANKS...

...to my wife, who helped edit the rough draft of this book in the midst of the often chaotic task of homemaking. Her patient, loving, hardworking example motivates me to be a better husband, father, preacher, and student of the Bible.

...to the people who offered sound advice, answered questions, broadened my thinking, challenged me, and caught additional typos, uncluding Vicky Yocum, Tony Clay, Caleb Colley, Glenn Colley, Jared Jackson, Dan Winkler, Justin Rogers, my dad, Brian Giselbach, among others.

TABLE OF CONTENTS

Note to teachers: If using this book in a class situation, it is recommended that you plan on devoting at least two or three class periods for each chapter.

FOREWORD

BY CALEB COLLEY

HUMAN beings can *know* God. This fact would be almost inconceivable if the Bible had not taught it. But the Bible does teach that we can know God, and so every Christian has made knowledge of God an overarching goal of life (2 Thess. 1:8; 1 John 4:8).

God also has provided the means for us to know Him, by giving us rationality and His revelation. As the first book in Ben's *You Are A Theologian* series explained, the Bible is God's perfect self-disclosure for humanity. We thus have at our fingertips the information that makes our knowledge of God possible. But anyone who has studied the Bible for any length of time has found that, in many ways, the Biblical doctrine of God is no simple matter. In fact, we can study the Bible for our whole lives and never stop learning new things about Him, and learning in greater detail how the various aspects of Biblical theology fit together. The study can be challenging.

Thankfully, in *You Are A Theologian: Thinking Right About God* we find a valuable tool for helping us know God through the Scriptures. The book you are about to read has many virtues. Among them are these:

- **Scriptural focus**. If you were to think of this book as an explanatory index to the Biblical doctrine of God, you would not be far off. The book certainly makes its own creative contribution, but it is full of Biblical passages and citations. Obviously, Ben intends to give us Biblical theology and not Giselbach's speculations. Thus the book ought to be used regularly in group Bible study.

- **Clarity and brevity**. Ben's writing style makes it possible for every reader to learn a great deal about God. Ben does not shy away from the necessary technical terminology, but he explains terms plainly and helpfully, and then fits them together. Words such as "sovereignty," "anthropomorphism," "immutability," and "monotheism" are helpful tools—useful, but only if we know what to do with them. Ben knows what to do with them, so he introduces us to complex truths and makes them our familiar friends. The longest chapter of this book concerns one of the most misunderstood subjects, the Trinity. One can learn more truth about the Trinity from these 22 pages than from many thick, trinitarian books combined.

- **Practicality**. Ben reminds us through many examples and illustrations that we must not only know facts about God, but know God personally and relationally. What we believe about God's attributes and activities will make a difference in how we relate to Him and how we live. This book portrays vividly many such implications, so that we are not left to wonder, "What difference does this make?" We have here a healthy emphasis on the proper use of God's gift of the freedom to choose.

- **Distinctiveness**. Ben defends the truth by exposing the weaknesses of many threats to Biblical theology including: Secularism, pluralism, Calvinism, pantheism, modalism, Arianism, tritheism, polytheism, feminism, atheism, egalitarianism, emergent theology, determinism, deism, materialism, and Pentecostalism. As we study this book, and the Scriptures it discusses, we may find ourselves (1) Changing our false beliefs; (2) Organizing and refining our true beliefs by understanding more precisely how they differ from false beliefs; (3) Preparing to better defend our true beliefs.

You Are a Theologian: Thinking Right About God offers deeper understanding of God, but also a framework in which to fit future study of the Bible and its theological truths. Is there a better reason to read a book?

PREFACE

THE purpose of the *You Are A Theologian* book series is to give Christians theological clarity and a solid foundation upon which to build their faith. We live in an age of skepticism, which means we must be all-the-more agile in our thinking of God's Word. There is an overabundance of Christians who are too spiritually feeble to take on even the weakest of attacks upon the Christian faith. We don't need any more of those kinds up people sitting in our pews. Instead, We need people who are eager to grow in the grace and knowledge of the Lord Jesus Christ. That requires us to be a *thinking* people. Let us think of ourselves as such.

Good theology begins with a proper understanding of God. You cannot go on to rightly divide the Word of truth if you do not first have an accurate knowledge of the Author. Much of false religion today can be traced to a warped view of God. If we do not know Him, we cannot know His doctrines.

We sometimes call the study of God "theology proper," for all other Biblical disciplines are second only to the study of God Himself. How you view God affects the foundation of every other area of study.

This book is not an apologetic work attempting to prove the existence of God. The Bible assumes the reality of God, thus we will assume the reader of this book already believes in Him as well. If you do not believe in God or have doubts about His existence, I would recommend the following books to you instead: *Reasons to Believe*, by Eric Lyons and Kyle Butt (2017), *Surveying the Evidence*, by Wayne Jackson, Eric Lyons, and Kyle Butt (2008), and *Always be Ready: Equipping Young People to Deal with Unbelief*, by Kyle Butt (2014).

You may notice that this book cites works by Christians (who range from faithful and unfaithful) and non-Christians alike. I reference them when I feel they bring value to a particular study. Please consider each citation based upon its own merit, and not as an endorsement of everything the individual teaches. Above all, be like the noble Bereans by studying everything you read in light of the Scriptures (cf. Acts 17:11).

This book is written with the idea that members will study this material throughout the week, and the teacher will discuss the questions and the key principles of the text during the assembly times. However, this book will also be very useful for personal study and growth. My hope is that you will find some of the issues discussed in this volume interesting and valuable. One of my favorite compliments I have received is, "Ben, you really made me think." Perhaps this book will make you think, hopefully in a way that is right.

In the hope of eternity with Him,

Ben Giselbach
August 7, 2017

CHAPTER 1

WHO IS GOD?

KNOWLEDGE OF GOD

MORE than 9 in 10 Americans believe in God.[1] All people everywhere have a deep, inner knowledge that God exists. Paul said that even the unbelieving pagans and secularists "knew God" but did not honor or even acknowledge Him (Rom. 1:21). Who could doubt God? Only a fool (Psa. 14:1; cf. Rom. 1:22).

Though God's existence is plain to everyone (Rom. 1:19), few people actually live for Him. Which means there are many more *practical* atheists (people who fail to acknowledge God in their lives) than there are *theoretical* atheists (people who intentionally disbelieve in God). In other words, people must willfully *reject* God and refuse to worship and live their lives for Him (Rom. 1:25) – it doesn't just happen by accident.

The question today is not, "Does God exist?" But "*What* God exists?" Nearly everyone believes in some sort of God. The issue at hand is not the existence of God but the *character* of God. Who is God? What is He like?

Just as the Bible makes no attempt to prove the existence of God, the Bible makes no attempt to give a concise definition of God. Perhaps the most specific description of Him is found in the conversation between the Lord and Moses at the place of the burning bush in the Sinai desert. Note their exchange:

> Then Moses said to God, "If I come to the people of Israel and say to

---

1 Frank Newport, *Gallup*

them, 'The God of your fathers has sent me to you,' and they ask me, 'What is His name?' what shall I say to them?" God said to Moses, "I AM WHO I AM." And He said, "Say this to the people of Israel, 'I AM has sent me to you.'" (Ex. 3:13-14).

This obscure description of God is evidence that a fully exhaustive definition of God is impossible for us. One of the reasons why the Israelites were prohibited from making any graven image of God (cf. Ex. 20:4) was surely because it was impossible to reduce God to a tangible, convenient image. Even after we have pieced together everything the Bible says about God, there will still be a great deal of mystery about Him. The Bible reminds us, "Oh, the depth of the riches and wisdom and knowledge of God! How unsearchable are His judgments and how inscrutable His ways!" (Rom. 11:33).

> *One of the reasons why the Israelites were prohibited from making any graven image of God was surely because it was impossible to reduce God to a tangible, convenient image.*

We must move beyond knowing He exists to knowing *Him* – His character and nature. The Bible says, "Whoever would draw near to God must believe that He exists and that He rewards those who seek Him" (Heb. 11:6). Thus, it is critically important to know Him as best we can. When we attempt to know Him better, we will find Him and be drawn into an even richer relationship with Him (Isa. 55:6; Matt. 7:7).

WE WILL NEVER KNOW *EVERYTHING* ABOUT GOD

In Job 11:7, two very important questions are asked: "Can you find out the *deep* things of God? Can you find out the *limit* of the Almighty?" To the first question, the answer is yes. If we truly want to know God, we will find Him. Why would God eternally punish those who do not know Him (2 Thess. 1:8) if it were not *possible* to know Him? Hebrews 8:11 tells us that God can be known. Paul said, "I know whom I have believed" (2 Tim. 1:12).

But what about the second question? Can we find out the *limit* of the Almighty? No, of course not! There is no limit to God. We can never exhaust our understanding of Him. Paul said, "How unsearchable are His judgments and how inscrutable His ways!" (Rom. 11:33). His love "surpasses knowledge" (Eph. 3:19), and His peace "surpasses all understanding" (Phil. 4:7). Isaiah declared, "His understanding is unsearchable" (Isa. 40:28) because "His understanding is infinite" (Psa. 147:5, NASB).

Our knowledge of God will always be limited. Why? Because we are *finite*, and He is *infinite*. Just as a 10-ounce glass of sweet tea cannot hold an infinite amount of sweet tea due to its finite volume (much to the dismay of many Southerners), the finite cannot grasp the infinite. God cannot be understood in His entirety. Again, the words of Paul echo in our ears, "Oh, the depth of the riches and wisdom and knowledge of God! How unsearchable are His judgments and how inscrutable His ways!" (Rom. 11:33).

In light of our *finitude* and God's ultimate *infinity*, we say God is **incomprehensible**. This does not mean we can never understand God; it just means we can never *fully* understand Him. Concerning His greatness, the Bible says, "His greatness is unsearchable" (Psa. 145:3). Concerning His understanding, the Bible says, "His understanding is beyond measure" (Psa. 147:5). Concerning His knowledge, David declares, "Such knowledge is too wonderful for me; it is high; I cannot attain it" (Psa. 139:6, cf. 17).

Paul implies God's *incomprehensibility* (and our utter dependence upon God's revelation to us) when he writes,

> ...these things God has revealed to us through the Spirit. For the Spirit searches everything, even the depths of God. For who knows a person's thoughts except the spirit of that person, which is in him? So also no one comprehends the thoughts of God except the Spirit of God. Now we have received not the spirit of the world, but the Spirit who is from God, that we might understand the things freely given us

by God. (1 Cor. 2:10-12)

The study of God is fascinating – one reason being that we can never know *too much* about God. We will never run out of things to learn about Him. We can unravel the mysteries of people, animals, and things – but we can never stop discovering God's greatness and majesty.

HOW CAN WE KNOW *ANYTHING* ABOUT GOD?

All of this begs the question: If God is incomprehensible, how then can we understand *anything* about Him?

By God's mercy, He has condescended to our language and spoken in ways we can understand (similar to how we might "coo" at a baby or use simple language when talking to a toddler). From the perspective of the throne of the infinite Creator of the Universe, we might even think of His words as a sort of "baby talk" to our vastly inferior human race. God has graciously stooped to our intellectual level to communicate information about Himself.

This is why God often speaks to us with metaphorical language. For example, God describes heaven as His "throne" and the earth as His "footstool" (Isa. 66:1) to teach us that He cannot be confined to a mere physical structure. But "throne" and "footstool" are not to be taken literally. God is not sitting on a physical throne like a human being would, nor is He actually kicking His feet on the planet earth (as if God, a Spirit-being, has physical feet!). God is also said to own "every beast of the forest" and all the "cattle on a thousand hills" (Psa. 50:10), but that does not mean we are to think of God literally as a cattle rancher. This kind of language simply illustrates that God is all-powerful and sovereign, and therefore He does not *need* animal sacrifices for His own benefit.

God is spirit (John 4:24). We, on the other hand, are stuck in physical bodies dwelling in a material world. The physical is all we know. Thus He must be described with physical metaphors so we can better understand His character. He is called a "rock" (1 Sam. 2:2), a "fortress" (Psalm 18:2), a "tower" (Prov. 18:10), and a "shield" (Gen. 15:1). He is even pictured as having the comforting wings of a bird (Psa. 57:1). These things are easier for us to imagine than a "spirit."

One specific type of metaphor is called an **anthropomorphism**, where God is described in human form. For example, the Bible mentions His eyes (e.g. Heb. 4:13), His hand (e.g. Ex. 7:5), His face (e.g. Num. 6:25), and His mouth (e.g. Psa. 33:6). The Bible also mentions God having emotional characteristics, a type of metaphor called an **anthropopathism**. For example, the Bible pictures God experiencing human-like feelings like grief (e.g. Eph. 4:30), regret (e.g. 1 Sam. 15:35), and jealousy (e.g. Ex. 20:5). Yet another type of metaphor is an **anthropoieses**, which portrays God with human actions. For example, the Bible says God "repented" (Gen. 6:6; Ex. 32:14, KJV), though the Bible also says in other places that God cannot technically change His mind (Mal. 3:6; Jas. 1:17; Num. 23:19). The unchangeableness of God is called His immutability. For further discussion on this attribute, turn to page 26.

As another example, the Bible also pictures God as being capable of forgetting (e.g. Isa. 43:25), something that is not technically possible for God in reality. God can "forget" in the sense that He can choose not to punish us for past sins (Heb. 8:12), but He cannot literally "forget" by deleting history from His memory. (Yet, when God says He forgets our sins, it is as sure as if He actually did forget.)

We need to be careful in interpreting metaphorical language; otherwise, we can be led into error or even into apostasy.

- If we believe that God literally "repented" (Exo. 32:14, KJV) and thus believe God somehow concluded that He was wrong in doing something, we can deny His immutability (see chapter 2).
- If we believe that God literally has physical eyes (Heb. 4:13), we can deny He is a spirit (John 4:24).
- If we believe that God literally "came down to see" (Gen. 11:5),

we can deny His omniscience (see chapter 2).

It is important for us to recognize that God describes Himself in human terms because that is often the only way we can begin to fathom *Him*. Do not make the mistake of taking metaphorical language literally. At the same time, we must also respect the reality that God did, in fact, use metaphorical terminology in revealing Himself to us, and therefore we must accept His words as no less true.

WE CAN KNOW ALL THAT IS NECESSARY

We need to be careful that we do not throw our hands in the air in desperation as we study God. Though we cannot know God *exhaustively*, we can still know things that are true about Him. We know that God is love (1 John 4:8), that He is light (1 John 1:5), and that He is righteous (Rom. 3:26) – even though our human nature may limit the degree to which we can appreciate these truths. To illustrate this point, imagine I tell you in conversation that I am married. Though I might not know everything about how women think (that's an understatement!), my statement that I am married is still entirely true. So it is with our knowledge of God. We can know true things about God — truths that should be precious to us (Psa. 139:17) — but we don't know everything.

God has revealed Himself to us and told us everything we need to know about Him (2 Tim. 3:15–17). This does not mean, however, that He told us every detail. God is just as wise in His reservations as He is in His revelations.

Wayne Grudem writes, "It is not true to say that God is unable to be understood, but it is true to say that He cannot be understood fully or exhaustively."[2] By His grace, God has revealed Himself to and told

2 Wayne Grudem, *Bible Doctrine*, p. 69

us everything that we need to know about Him (2 Tim. 3:15-17). This does not mean, however, that He told us every detail. God is just as wise in His reservations as He is in His revelations. We simply need to follow Him, as a child naturally trusts his father (Luke 18:17; Matt. 18:3; 19:14). Bear in mind, "the secret things belong to the Lord our God, but the things that are revealed belong to us and to our children forever, that we may do all the words of this Law" (Deut. 29:29). Many of the things He does are things we can never understand (Job 37:5). But we have heard His "whisper" (Job 26:14). While we cannot know Him perfectly (Job 11:7), we can know enough to be fully equipped to love, worship, obey, and spend eternity with Him.

WE COME TO *KNOW* GOD WHEN WE COME TO *UNDERSTAND* GOD

The more we know *about* God, the more we come to know Him personally. Jeremiah says,

> Thus says the Lord: "Let not the wise man boast in his wisdom, let not the mighty man boast in his might, let not the rich man boast in his riches, but let him who boasts boast in this, that he understands and *knows me*, that I am the Lord who practices steadfast love, justice, and righteousness in the earth. For in these things I delight, declares the Lord." (Jer. 9:23-24, emp. added)

How comforting it is that, despite our limited intellectual capability, we can still know God!

In other words, we should not look for joy in our abilities or possessions, but in knowing the Lord Himself. Jesus says, "And this is eternal life, that they know you the only true God, and Jesus Christ whom you have sent" (John 17:3, emp. added). John says Jesus came so that we may "know Him who is true" (1 John 5:20). Jesus left His spirit with His apostles so they could write facts about God and we, in turn, can "know Him" (1 John 2:13). How comforting it is that, despite our limited intellectual capability, we can still know God!

WHAT WE TALK ABOUT WHEN WE TALK ABOUT GOD

Because of the limits of human language, it is often difficult to describe God. But we are not without at least *some* tools to help us better understand Him.

One way we describe God is by describing what He is not. For example, when we say God is *infinite*, we mean God is "not finite" (meaning He has no limit). When we say God is *immutable*, we mean God is "not mutable" (meaning He does not change). In contrast, human beings change over time and eventually die because human beings are finite and mutable.

Another way we describe God is by describing Him in terms of His ultimate greatness. When we do this, we take terms that are familiar to us and we take them to the utmost degree. For example, we are familiar with the words "power" and "knowledge." In reference to God's power and knowledge, God possesses these qualities to the utmost degree, so we attach to them the word "omni." God is *omnipotent*, with *omni* added to the Latin word *potentia*, meaning "power." God is *omniscient*, with *omni* added to the Latin word *scientia*, meaning "knowledge."

Yet another way we talk about God is by making direct, absolute statements about His character, such as "God is holy," "God is sovereign," "God is love." We know these characteristics belong primarily to God and thus we affirm they belong to Him in the ultimate sense.

WHY KNOWING GOD IS SO CRITICALLY IMPORTANT

There are several reasons why we must concern ourselves with understanding God accurately:

1. WE CANNOT RECOGNIZE FALSE GODS AND BELIEFS WITHOUT KNOWING THE TRUE GOD

Virtually every major spiritual belief is a consequence of our understanding of God.

- The conviction that the Bible is the Word of God and that Jesus is the Son of God is based entirely on what we mean by *God*.
- Our understanding of miracles and providence is based upon our understanding of the *sovereignty* of God.
- Our view of eschatology (the study of the end-times) is dependent upon the *omnipotence* and *infallibility* of God.
- Our view of hell is dependent upon the absolute *justice* of God.

If we do not understand God accurately, it will hurt our ability to understand the *rest* of what the Bible teaches. Furthermore, the Bible frequently warns us about the danger of false teachers and prophets (Matt. 7:15; 2 Cor. 11:4; Gal. 1:8; 1 Tim. 4:1; 1 John 4:1). But you cannot recognize *error* and falsehood without first knowing what is *true*. A counterfeit cannot be spotted without first knowing what is authentic. Likewise, you cannot know what is *false* about God and His Word without first knowing what is *true* about Him. We must come to know God if we want to grow in – and defend – the faith (Phil. 1:7; 1 Pet. 3:15; Jude 3).

2. WE CANNOT GROW CLOSER TO GOD WITHOUT A FIRM UNDERSTANDING OF GOD

I believe that ignorance of God – ignorance of His attributes, His ways, and how to walk with Him – is the cause of much of the church's weakness today. A. W. Tozer said, "What you think of God is the most important thing about you."[3] It is a fact that you will never surpass the god you serve, nor will you ever rise above who you believe to be

---

3 A.W. Tozer, *The Knowledge of the Holy*, p. 1

Supreme. The reason there are so many Christians who are stunted in their spiritual growth is because they are stunted in their thoughts about God.

What you think of God will have an obvious practical effect on how you live your life. Furthermore, "it is a psychological fact that we tend to become like what (or whom) we admire the most."[4] Over time, it becomes obvious where your affections lie. Your holiness and righteousness will conform to the level of the God you worship. J.I. Packer writes, "Nothing will so enlarge the intellect, nothing so magnify the whole soul of man, as a devout, earnest, continued investigation of the great subject of the Deity."[5]

3. WE CANNOT COME TO KNOW GOD WITHOUT FIRST KNOWING ABOUT GOD

It is important that we do not study God for the sole purpose of gaining academic knowledge about Him. After all, why is it that some of the most intelligent of people are often the most distant from God? As Paul told the Corinthians, "Knowledge puffs up... If anyone imagines that he knows something, he does not yet know as he ought to know" (1 Cor. 8:1-2). Self-satisfaction in our own understanding of God is not what we are seeking.

Studying about God must be our means to the end of ultimately knowing God personally. In other words, our knowledge of God must not be a mere *theoretical* pursuit; it must be a *practical* one. Is this not what the psalmist wanted? "Blessed are those who keep His testimonies;" "teach me Your statutes;" "My soul is consumed with longing for Your rules at all times;" "How sweet are Your words to my taste" (Psa. 119:2, 12, 20, 103). However, notice there was *purpose* behind the psalmist's pursuit of God: loving God and knowing Him personally. "I will keep Your statutes;" "I will run in the way of Your commandments;" "I incline my heart to perform Your statutes

---

4 Norman Geisler, *Systematic Theology*, p. 408
5 J.I. Packer, *Knowing God*, p. 18

forever, to the end;" "let no iniquity get dominion over me;" "I do Your commandments;" "My soul keeps Your testimonies;" (Psa. 119:8, 32, 112, 133, 166, 167). The psalmist valued knowledge about God simply as a means to the ultimate end of knowing God personally.

Knowing God is more than gaining knowledge about Him, but it is certainly not less. We must seek knowledge of what the Bible teaches if we are to know God personally.

Sadly, unlike the noble psalmist, there is a great deal of contempt today for the idea of seeking knowledge about God in the Bible. For example, Max Lucado made the clumsy statement, "God rewards those who seek Him. Not those who seek doctrine of religion or systems or creeds."[6] This kind of statement sounds nice at first, but is nonsensical upon closer scrutiny. We must recognize that it is *impossible* to seek God without seeking doctrine and systems about Him in the Bible. Our goal in studying about God must be to walk *with* Him and learn *how* to love Him more faithfully. Doctrine and systems are indispensable in our search for God.

CONCLUSION

Even though we can never possess exhaustive knowledge about God, we can still know Him personally and speak about Him in meaningful ways. God has talked to us and revealed Himself to us in our terms, and – because we are made in His image and thus share His spirit likeness (Gen. 1:26-27) – we can enjoy thinking about Him in ways He has communicated to us.

In 1962 at the University of Chicago, a student asked the late Karl Barth (who many regard to be one of the most influential religious thinkers of the 20th century) what he believed to have been the most momentous theological discovery of his life. Barth's simple answer was, "Jesus loves me, this I know, for the Bible tells me so."[7] Some

---

6   Max Lucado, *Grace For The Moment*, p. 361
7   Joseph Mangina, *Karl Barth: Theologian of Christian Witness*, p. 9

laughed at his answer, thinking he was joking. But after a few moments of silence passed, the audience realized his answer was serious. Our study of God – and *all* of theology for that matter – should cause us to recognize His magnificent greatness, our ultimate insignificance in comparison, and the wonder of God's grace in light of His love for us.

The breathtaking truth about God is this: "For God so loved the world, that He gave His only Son" (John 3:16). As we think more about God, we stand in awe at the fact that such a Supreme Being would make such a great sacrifice for us.

DISCUSSION QUESTIONS

1. Is atheism something that happens by accident?

2. Is it possible to fully understand God? Why or why not?

3. What do we mean when we say that God is **incomprehensible**?

4. What illustration would you give someone to better explain how our *finite* minds cannot understand an *infinite* God?

5. What are some different types of metaphors that God uses to explain Himself to us?

6. When reading metaphorical descriptions of God, what is the difference between understanding them literally and understanding them as true?

7. What are some of the dangers of understanding metaphorical language about God literally?

8. Why is it so important to know God?

9. Why do you think so many Christians are experiencing stunted spiritual growth?

10. Is it possible to know God personally without knowing about God through His Word? Why or why not?

CHAPTER 2

TO INFINITY, AND BEYOND

GOD'S INCOMMUNICABLE ATTRIBUTES

IF I asked you to describe yourself, what would you say? Perhaps you would talk about your physical characteristics – your height, gender, skin color, eye color, hair color, etc. You might tell me about your marital status, career, religion, or hobbies. These characteristics are what make you, well, *you*. Even if some of these things changed – maybe you switched jobs, got a new hobby, dyed your hair – you would pretty much still be the same old *you*.

This is not true when it comes to knowing God. God *is* His attributes. If any of His attributes changed, He would cease being God. There is no difference between God's attributes and God's essence. We cannot strip God of His attributes only to find a more simplified being. In fact, we cannot even strip God of just one of His attributes without taking away His very *Godhood*. For instance, if we took away God's omniscience or His omnipotence, He would cease to be God.

GOD IS ACTUALLY QUITE SIMPLE

We should recognize the fact that God – as incomprehensible as He seems to us – is actually very simple in terms of what makes Him God. God cannot be divided into parts. Even though human beings have different personal attributes and body parts – fingers, arms, legs, ears, and so forth – God does not. We call this God's **simplicity**; God is not complex. All of God's attributes put together make God who He is. He is simple in that He cannot be divided and His attributes cannot be compartmentalized.

God's simplicity means that His attributes define each other. For example, when we say God is patient, eternal, loving, righteous, and merciful, we are saying these attributes describe His other attributes. God is *patiently* omnipotent, *lovingly* omnipotent, *righteously* omnipotent, and *mercifully* omnipotent. He *eternally* patient, *eternally* loving, *eternally* righteous, and *eternally* merciful. The same is true with His love, righteousness, mercy, etc. Each attribute of God is equally important, and each attribute defines the other.

Recognizing God's simplicity helps us better understand the difference between God and humanity. Unlike any of God's creatures, His attributes perfectly and uniformly define one another. And unlike any of God's creatures, His attributes cannot be separated from one another.

GOD HAS COMMUNICABLE & INCOMMUNICABLE ATTRIBUTES

Sometimes we make a distinction between God's **communicable** and His **incommunicable** attributes. Something that is *communicable* can be transferred from one person to the other. If you have the flu, you are probably contagious and thus should temporarily stay away from other people (unless you really don't like them[1]). Diseases like the flu can be transmitted to other people and thus we say they are *communicable*. Likewise, God's communicable attributes (e.g. *love, holiness, grace*, etc.) are attributes that can be at least partially transmitted to human beings. This description isn't perfect. God's communicable attributes can't be completely communicated. We will never be perfectly loving – or holy – or gracious. But nonetheless, God does share these qualities with us to some degree.

On the other hand, God's *incommunicable* attributes are those that cannot be imitated by His creatures. Even God Himself cannot transfer His incommunicable attributes to someone else. Such would be logically impossible. For example, it would be impossible for God

---

1 I kid, I kid.

to create another God. If He did, the so-called new God would just be a created being and thus would lack the necessary attributes that only God can possess, such as His *aseity*, *eternality*, and *immutability*.

Let's look at some of God's incommunicable attributes:

ASEITY (SELF-EXISTENT)

As a teenager, I couldn't wait to have independence. As soon as state law allowed, I wanted a driver's license and a car. I wanted to be my own person and do whatever I wanted. But like most other teenagers, I never achieved true independence. I still had to ask my parents for money, they still had to sign legal documents (since I was underage), and I still had to sleep and eat somewhere (and I wasn't about to do my own laundry!). Somehow I survived the injustice of it all.

Unlike God, human beings can never be truly independent. To exist, we must first be created, and then we must depend on our environment for our continued survival. We need air to breathe and food to eat. We are often at the mercy of other people as it relates to our health and safety. God, on the other hand, is not dependent upon anything. He is eternal, self-existent, self-sufficient, and has the power of being in and of itself. We call this God's **aseity**, from the Latin *aseite*, meaning "of oneself."

God does not need anything. Paul said to the pagans in Athens:

> The God who made the world and everything in it, being Lord of heaven and earth, does not live in temples made by man, nor is He served by human hands, as though He needed anything, since He Himself gives to all mankind life and breath and everything. (Acts 17:24-25)

Implied is the fact that God does not depend on man. Rather, we depend entirely on Him. Our very existence is purely an act of grace.

Some believe that God made humanity because He was lonely and needed someone to keep Him company. This is entirely wrong because

> *God is fundamentally different than everyone or everything else. He is the Creator; all else is merely created. He is perfect and complete; all else is limited and imperfect.*

such a case would mean that God *needed* to create someone else in order to be happy or fulfilled. Yet God is completely independent of His creation. He does not need us.

However, the Bible says that God is love (1 John 4:8), and love cannot exist without an object for that love. Who, then, did God love before He created mankind? Jesus told us the answer when He prayed, "Father, glorify me in your own presence with the glory that I had with you before the world existed" (John 17:5). Then He prayed about His glory that God had given Him "because [God] loved [Him] before the foundation of the world" (John 17:24). This means the Father and the Son had love and togetherness before the Universe was created, and thus God never had any sort of emotional need for mankind.

Note the Biblical basis for God's aseity:

- **No one can thwart God's work**. God said in Isaiah 43:12-13: "I am God. Even from eternity I am He, and there is none who can deliver out of my hand; I act and who can reverse it?" (NASB).
- **God is totally free to act according to His Will**. He always has been and always will be. Moses says, "Before the mountains were brought forth, or ever you had formed the earth and the world, from everlasting to everlasting you are God" (Psa 90:2).
- **A self-existent God is the only possible explanation for the creation of the universe**. "For you created all things, and by your will they existed and were created" (Rev. 4:11).

God exists in an infinitely stronger and better way than anything else in the universe. God is not merely "bigger" than us. It is inadequate to compare man with God using illustrations like a drop of water compared to the ocean, an anthill compared to a mountain, a speck of dust compared to a planet, or a candlestick compared to the sun. God is *fundamentally* different than us. He is the Creator; all else is merely made. He is perfect and complete; all else is limited and imperfect. Everything else could pass away in an instant, and God would be no less God.

When thinking about God's aseity, we must guard against the temptation to view ourselves as not having any meaning. Is there any meaning or purpose behind our existence? The Bible teaches that mankind brings God joy. God created us and has given us meaning. Concerning every human being ever created, "Everyone who is called by my name, whom I created for my glory, whom I formed and made" (Isa. 43:7). Even though God was under no obligation to create us, He decided to do so that we might glorify Him (cf. Eph. 1:11-12; Rev. 4:11). We find our value in God. When we live for God, we find our true worth. On the other hand, when we depart from God's Will for our life, we are forfeiting our very purpose for existence. There is no value apart from God.

Meaning is only found in God. God has given us the capacity to bring Him real joy and pleasure. While God does not need us for anything, perhaps the most awesome fact is that God in His free will decided to delight in us. Isaiah declares, "You shall be a crown of beauty in the hand of the Lord, and a royal diadem in the hand of your God" (Isa. 62:3). To be valuable to God makes us more valuable than all the riches in the world.

ETERNALITY (BEYOND TIME)

"Every good thing must come to an end," as the saying goes. Vacations; cheeseburgers; spring breaks; that TV show you've been binge watching on Netflix; etc. Everything that has a beginning must come to an end, including the Apple Care Protection Plan for my MacBook. And I assure you, it won't be very long until I run out of the Cookies & Crème Blue Bell ice cream currently sitting in my fridge.

But God has no beginning or end. He has no past, present, or future – He simply always has been and always will be. Sometimes a child will ask, "Who made God?" The answer: *no one*; God is the eternal I AM (cf. John 8:58). There was never a point in time when God did not exist.

God is infinite. When we apply this to time, we call this God's **eternality**. Because language is inherently bound by time (we describe things in *past*, *present*, and *future* tenses), there are limits to how we can describe God's eternality. It is impossible for us to fully wrap our minds around the true meaning of *eternity*. Nonetheless, God in His revelation has exhausted the limits of language in describing His eternality.

God is *bigger* than time – He is *beyond* time. As Isaiah says, God "inhabits eternity" (Isa. 57:15). The very first verse of the Bible says, "In the beginning, God created the heavens and the earth" (Gen. 1:1). Modern science has found that time cannot exist without the universe. Thus, since God is *before* the universe, He transcends time itself. Hebrews tells us that, through Christ, God "created the world" (Heb. 1:2). In that verse, the Greek word for "world," *aiōnas*, does not refer to the physical world, but rather the unfolding of time itself.

Note the Biblical basis for God's eternality:

- **In Jesus' prayer in the garden of Gethsemane, we find a glimpse of the eternal Trinity[2] before time itself when He said; "…glorify me in your own presence with the glory that I had with you before the world existed" (John 17:5).**
- **Paul spoke of the "grace which [God] gave us in Christ Jesus before the ages began" (2 Tim. 1:9).**
- **Paul also said that God promised eternal life "before the ages began" (Titus 1:2).**
- **Christ, because He is eternal, brought the temporal world into existence (John 1:3; Col. 1:16).**

---

2 Chapter 4

- **God always has been and always will be God.** Psalm 90:2 says, "Before the mountains were brought forth, or ever you had formed the earth and the world, from everlasting to everlasting you are God." "'I am the Alpha and the Omega,' says the Lord God, 'who is and who was and who is to come, the Almighty'" (Rev. 1:8).
- **God was working "before the foundation of the world"** (Eph. 1:4).
- **Jude says that "glory, majesty, dominion, and authority" have belonged to God since "before all time and now and forever"** (Jude 25).
- **First Corinthians 2:7 says God decreed the wisdom spoken by the apostles "before the ages for our glory."**

Simply put, God *always has been* (cf. Ex. 3:14; John 8:58). Because God created "the ages" (Heb. 1:2) and is "before the ages" (1 Cor. 2:7), God is not bound by time. He sees every event, regardless of the point in time, with equal clarity.

All of time is to God as if it just happened. No event ever leaves God's consciousness.

Psalm 90:4 says, "For a thousand years in your sight are but as yesterday when it is past, or as a watch in the night" (cf. 2 Pet. 3:8). This is a figurative way of saying that all of time is to God as if it just happened. No event ever leaves God's consciousness. God sees and knows everything that has ever happened and ever will happen with equal vividness.

OMNISCIENCE (ALL-KNOWING)

What would happen if you knew *everything* about the future? You could win the lottery *every* time (not that a Christian would ever play the lottery). You could save countless lives knowing when and where the next tornado, earthquake, terrorist attack, fire, or mass shooting is going to occur. You could quickly become a billionaire by investing every last penny into the next successful startup company. And, of course, you would always know when the "Hot Now" sign at Krispy Kreme is about to be turned on.

God is infinite. When we apply this to knowledge, we call it God's **omniscience**. Understanding God's omniscience is pretty straightforward: God knows everything – yesterday, today, and tomorrow. Remember, God is infinite in His nature, and since His knowledge is also His nature, it follows that God must also have infinite knowledge. God knows everything about the past, the present, and the future. If He didn't know everything, He would be limited in His knowledge and thus wouldn't be God. "Limited omniscience" is, after all, an oxymoron.

Note the Biblical basis of God's omniscience:

- **God has limitless knowledge.** The psalmist says that God's "understanding is beyond measure" (Psa. 147:5). "Even before a word is on my tongue, behold, O Lord, you know it altogether" (Psa. 139:4). Job asks, "Will any teach God knowledge?" (Job 21:22).
- **God knows everything about His creation.** He knows every star in the universe (Psa. 147:4). He knows every animal in the world (Psa. 50:11). Jesus says, "Are not two sparrows sold for a penny? And not one of them will fall to the ground apart from your Father" (Matt. 10:29).
- **God knows the works of every person.** He "observes all their deeds" (Psa. 33:15). "No creature is hidden from His sight, but all are naked and exposed to the eyes of Him to whom we must give account" (Heb. 4:13; cf. Ecc. 12:14).
- **God knows the heart of every person.** He says, "For I know the things that come into your mind" (Eze. 11:5). "I the Lord search the heart and test the mind" (Jer. 17:10). "The Lord searches all hearts and understands every plan and thought" (1 Chron. 28:9).

- **God knows all of our needs.** Jesus says, "Your Father knows what you need before you ask Him" (Matt. 6:8).
- **God knows the future.** "Behold, the former things have come to pass, and new things I now declare; before they spring forth I tell you of them" (Isa. 42:9). "I am God, and there is none like me, declaring the end from the beginning and from ancient times things not yet done" (Isa. 46:9-10).

It boggles the mind when we seriously think about God's omniscience as it relates to future events. Hippolytus, an early Christian from the late second century, said that God "is fully acquainted with whatever is about to take place, for foreknowledge also is present to Him."[3] Tertullian, another early Christian from the second century, said "it was by this very attribute that He foreknew all things when He appointed them their places, and appointed them their places when He foreknew them."[4]

OMNIPRESENCE (EVERYWHERE)

God did not just create the universe only to walk away. No, God is ever present and active in our daily lives. "In Him we live and move and have our being" (Acts 17:28). Because God is present everywhere, we can have a real relationship with Him. He knows everything about us – better than we even know ourselves. Jesus said, "When you pray, go into your room and shut the door and pray to your Father who is in secret. And your Father who sees in secret will reward you" (Matt. 6:6).

God is infinite. When we apply this to space, we call it God's **omnipresence.** God is everywhere, all the time. To put it another way, there is nowhere that God is absent. Walter Conner writes,

> The omnipresence of God has reference to God's immanence in the spatial and temporal order, and means that He is immanent in that order at all points of time and space. The omnipresence of God means that He is everywhere present in space and time. There is no point of

---

3 Hippolytus, *Ante-Nicene Fathers* (Vol. 5), p. 150
4 Tertullian, *Ante-Nicene Fathers* (Vol. 3), p. 301

space, no moment of time, where God is not present.[5]

David declares:

> Where shall I go from your Spirit? Or where shall I flee from your presence? If I ascend to heaven, you are there! If I make my bed in Sheol, you are there! If I take the wings of the morning and dwell in the uttermost parts of the sea, even there your hand shall lead me, and your right hand shall hold me. (Psalm 139:7-10)

It is important that we understand what God's omnipresence does *not* mean. It does not mean that God *is* creation, which is the doctrine of **pantheism**. The Bible clearly teaches that God *made* the world; He is not the world Himself. Omnipresence also does not mean that God is *in* creation, which is the doctrine of **panentheism**. God does not dwell within – nor is He bound by – space, time, or matter as humans do, since the Bible teaches that God is spirit. Paul Helm writes, "God does not fill space; rather, He is spaceless – outside of space and yet in full control of everything that occurs in space as well as in time."[6]

There is, of course, a sense in which God is *in* the universe because He caused creation (cf. Col. 1:16). Yet God is not *in* the universe as part of the *effect* of creation. Norman Geisler further defines God's omnipresence for us:

> God is everywhere at once. As the indivisible Being, God does not have *one part here* and *another part there,* for He has no parts. God is *present* to but not *part of* creation. God is *everywhere,* but He is not *any thing.* He is *at every point in space,* but He is not *spatial.* He is *at every point in space,* but He is not *of* any point in space.[7]

Does that make total sense to you? I didn't think so. It hurts my brain, too. But we must accept what the Bible teaches without demanding to first fully understand every detail. This is the definition of faith.

King Solomon understood the futility of thinking that God could literally dwell within a man-made temple when he said, "But will God

---

5 Walter Conner, *Revelation and God*, p. 233
6 Paul Helm, *God Under Fire*, p. 12
7 Norman Geisler, *Systematic Theology*, p. 493

indeed dwell on the earth? Behold, heaven and the highest heaven cannot contain you; how much less this house that I have built! (1 Kings 8:27). Paul again reminded us that God "does not live in temples made by man" (Acts 17:24). Jeremiah writes:

> Am I a God at hand, declares the Lord, and not a God far away? Can a man hide himself in secret places so that I cannot see him? declares the Lord. Do I not fill heaven and earth? declares the Lord. (Jer. 23:23-24)

As the Creator, God possesses infinite knowledge about everything He has created. "In Him all things hold together" (Col. 1:17). The Son "is the radiance of the glory of God and the exact imprint of His nature, and He upholds the universe by the word of His power" (Heb. 1:3). "Worthy are you, our Lord and God, to receive glory and honor and power, for you created all things, and by your will they existed and were created" (Rev. 4:11).

God is present everywhere. Because God is the infinite Creator, He cannot be contained within His creation. It would be more accurate, actually, to say that creation is in God. Because God has no "parts," every part of God is present everywhere.

> *Because God is the infinite Creator, He cannot be contained within His creation. It would be more accurate, actually, to say that creation is in God.*

OMNIPOTENCE (ALL-POWERFUL)

"Is anything too hard for the Lord?" (Gen. 18:14), asks the Lord rhetorically. Jeremiah answers the question. "Ah, Lord God! It is you who have made the heavens and the earth by your great power and by your outstretched arm! Nothing is too hard for you" (Jer. 32:17).

When we apply God's infinity to power, we call it God's **omnipotence**. Put another way, there is nothing the Lord cannot do. He is all-powerful. There are no limits to what He can do according to His will and good pleasure. Jesus says, "With God, all things are possible" (Matt. 19:26). Paul reminds us that God "is able to do far more abundantly than all that we ask or think" (Eph. 3:20). God's power and ability is infinite.

Frank Chesser describes God's omnipotence this way:

> There is nothing that is right and in harmony with His Will that God cannot do. It is foolish to think that God who created the universe with all of its elements in six days could be limited in power. He could have done so in six seconds had He so desired. Can man, with his frail, feeble, diminutive mental capacity comprehend such power?[8]

However, God cannot do that which is contradictory. In other words, God cannot create a square circle or a rock too large for Him to move. He also cannot do that which is contradictory to His nature. For example, He cannot lie (Titus 1:2; Heb. 6:18), He cannot deny Himself (2 Tim. 2:13), He cannot be tempted (Jas. 1:13), and He cannot force people to *freely* obey Him (Matt. 23:37).

Furthermore, just because God is all-powerful does not mean He must always *exercise* His power. For example, God easily had the power to destroy the universe when mankind crucified Christ (cf. Matt. 26:53-54), and He would have been entirely righteous in doing so. Yet, God is free to limit the use of His power while still maintaining the infinite extent of His power.

God cannot do that which is contradictory.

IMMUTABLE (UNCHANGEABLE)

It is often difficult for us today to relate to people who lived in the Near East thousands of years ago. The people and events recorded in the Bible are geographically, culturally, technologically, and politically distant from us. We live in the space age, with smartphones, air-conditioning, and Pop-tarts. They lived in a brutal, primitive, pre-

---

8 Frank Chesser, *Thinking Right About God*, p. 23

industrial world.

When we read about God dealing with Adam, Abraham, Moses, David, and all the other great Biblical characters, we see how God interacted with them. We see prophets rebuking idolatry and threatening God's severe judgment in response to sin. We find the Son of God performing miracles and conversing with Jews and Samaritans, Pharisees and Sadducees, and then being crucified for them. We read letters by the apostles of Jesus addressing strange problems and heresies in the church back then that we do not have to deal with today.

Their world and our world seem entirely different. So how is the Bible relevant to us today? The answer is in God Himself. The God the people in the Bible had to deal with is the same God we must deal with today. God is exactly the same today as He was 2,000- 4,000- 6,000 years ago. God has not changed. What makes the ancient words of Holy Writ applicable to us today is God's **immutability**.

God is unchangeable in His nature and attributes. We would expect this from a God who is self-existent (aseity) and eternal. He is the great "I AM" (Exodus 3:14), the One who is always the same. The Bible says both God the Father and God the Son never change (Psa. 102:25-27; Heb. 13:8). "For I the LORD do not change" (Mal. 3:6). James reminds us that with God "there is no variation or shadow due to change" (Jas. 1:17). The Hebrews author talks of "the immutability of His counsel" and of "two immutable things, in which it was impossible for God to lie" (Heb. 6:17-18, KJV). "God is not man, that He should lie, or a son of man, that He should change His mind" (Num. 23:19).

As J.I. Packer summarizes,

> The answer to the child's question "Who made God?" is simply that God did not need to be made, for He was always there. He exists forever, and He is always the same. He does not grow older. His life does not wax or wane. He does not gain new powers nor lose those that He once had. He does not mature or develop. He does not get

stronger, or weaker, or wiser, as time goes by.[9]

CAN GOD CHANGE HIS MIND?

When we say that God never changes, we should clarify that He never changes in His nature, attributes, and purpose. However, God is not unchangeable in ways many think Him to be. Throughout the Bible, we find a God who acts differently based upon different situations. For instance, God did not destroy Nineveh as He promised when the citizens repented (Jonah 3:4, 10). God spared Israel when Moses intervened, begging Him not to consume the nation (Ex. 32:9-14). God added another fifteen years to Hezekiah's life after hearing his prayer (Isa. 38:1-6).

Because God is also just and righteous, the way He interacts with man depends on the present state of man's heart. Wayne Grudem explains,

> These instances should all be understood as true expressions of God's present attitude or intention with respect to the situation as it exists at that moment. If the situation changes, then of course God's attitude or expression of intention will also change. This is just saying that God responds differently to different situations.[10]

Throughout the Bible, we find a God who is consistent in His nature, attributes, and purpose. If God did not respond differently when mankind changes, He would cease to be *merciful* and *just* – which would be impossible, since God and His attributes are immutable.

DOES GOD FEEL EMOTIONS?

Some people go too far in discussions about God's immutability and teach that God does not have passions or emotions. In other words, they incorrectly argue that God is **impassible**, meaning He is not subject to passions.

9   J.I. Packer, *Knowing God*, p. 77
10 Wayne Grudem, *Bible Doctrine*, p. 74

Of course, God does not have *sinful* passions or emotions, such as lust or envy. Yet the notion that God does not have *any* feelings or emotions conflicts with the Bible, I believe. In fact, since we are made in the image of God (Gen. 1:26-27) and experience passions and emotions, it logically follows that God also experiences emotions. Emotions are how conscious, intelligent beings respond rationally. Among other things, God is capable of anger (Ex. 32:10; Psa. 7:11; Rom. 1:18), He rejoices (Isa. 62:5; Jer. 32:41), He feels jealousy (Ex. 20:5; Josh. 24:19), He is grieved (Gen. 6:6; Psa. 78:40; Eph. 4:30), He loves (Isa. 54:8; Psa. 103:17; John 3:16), and He feels compassion (Psa. 135:14; Deut. 32:36; Matt. 9:36).

If God does not have emotions, then the fact that Jesus – who is the "exact representation" of God's being" (Heb. 1:3) – wept at Lazarus's tomb (John 11:35) has no meaning and thus offers us no hope. I'm so thankful that God feels compassion for His children (Psa. 103:13). We serve a God with passions we are to imitate – hating sin and loving righteousness (cf. Heb. 1:9).

CONCLUSION

God's incommunicable attributes are the reason we praise Him. He is so utterly unlike us – in His self-existence, eternality, omniscience, omnipotence, omnipresence, and changeableness. Professional athletes and musical performers receive overwhelming fanfare and are sometimes paid millions of dollars. But they will be forgotten within the next generation or two, and someone else will break their record or replace their popularity. However, we owe our innermost gratitude and everlasting worship to the One upon whom everyone of us is absolutely dependent. No one ultimately deserves our praise like the One who has created the universe.

DISCUSSION QUESTIONS

1. Can God be divided into parts?

2. What is the difference between God's **communicable** and **incommunicable** attributes?

3. What is God's **aseity**?

4. Does God *need* humanity?

5. What is God's **infinity**?

6. How would you answer the child's question, "Who made God?"

7. What does it mean when we say God is **omniscient, omnipotent, and omnipresent**?

8. Is there anything that God *cannot* do?

9. What is God's **immutability**?

10. Can God change His mind? Give proof for your answer.

CHAPTER 3

YOU'RE THE SPITTIN' IMAGE... WELL, SORT OF

GOD'S COMMUNICABLE ATTRIBUTES

GOD never says, "You shall therefore be eternal and self-existent, for I am eternal and self-existent," or, "You shall therefore be immutable, for I am immutable." He does, however, say, "You shall therefore be holy, for I am holy" (Lev. 11:45).

We are commanded to imitate God. While there are attributes of God that we can never imitate, such as God's *aseity, omniscience,* and *omnipresence,* there are some attributes that can be reflected in humanity, such as *holiness, justice, love,* and *goodness.* The apostle Paul writes, "Therefore be imitators of God, as beloved children. And walk in love, as Christ loved us and gave Himself up for us, a fragrant offering and sacrifice to God" (Eph. 5:1-2). Thus it logically follows that there are certain attributes of God that are possible for us to at least somewhat exemplify. These are called **communicable** attributes.

The more you grow in the Christian faith, the more these attributes will become part of you. Christians are people who are trying to be like God. Jesus commands, "You therefore must be perfect, as your heavenly Father is perfect" (Matt. 5:48). The word translated here as "perfect," *teleios,* means "complete" or "mature." In other words, God is the standard by which we must measure ourselves. Therefore, to be like God, we must understand what He is like.

However, in the religious world today, there is a strange belief that God cannot ever be truly understood. Rob Bell goes much too far when he remarks, "The moment God is figured out with nice neat lines and definitions, we are no longer dealing with God. We are dealing with somebody we made up."[1] This statement is misleading, because Scripture does in fact give us very concrete truths about God. If there weren't any "lines and definitions" about God in the Bible, then Jesus' command for Christians to "be perfect, as your heavenly Father is perfect" leaves us hopeless. Of course, as David Lipscomb correctly observes, "If a man must understand all that is said in reference to God in the Bible before he can serve Him, no one will be saved."[2] But there are some things we *must* know about God when we become Christians, and – as we walk with the Lord – we will know Him and His attributes with increasing clarity.

Let us now note some of His communicable attributes:

HOLINESS

Holy means sacred, apart, righteous, separate, or transcendent. Something that is holy is cut off and separated from that which is common. The Bible speaks of holy ground (Ex. 3:5), holy assemblies (Ex. 12:16), holy Sabbaths (Ex. 16:23), a holy nation (Ex. 19:6; 1 Pet. 2:9), holy men (Ex. 22:31), holy garments (Ex. 35:21), a holy crown (Lev. 8:9), a holy linen coat (Lev. 16:4), holy houses (Lev. 27:14), holy tithes (Lev. 27:30), a holy ark (2 Chron. 35:3), a holy city (Neh. 11:18), a holy mountain (Psa. 99:9), holy promises (Psa. 105:42), holy women (1 Pet. 3:5), holy brothers (Heb. 3:1), a holy kiss (2 Cor. 13:12), holy hands (1 Tim. 2:8), holy Scriptures (2 Tim. 3:15), and a holy faith (Jude 20). Anything or anyone that is separated from the secular world and dedicated to God can be said to be holy.

God's holiness means that God is separate from all that is not God.

But what does it mean when we say *God* is holy? What can you

1 Rob Bell, *Velvet Elvis*, p. 10
2 David Lipscomb, *Queries and Answers*, p. 191

possibly separate from God to make Him more holy? To say that God is holy means God is separate from all that is not God.

If a man is holy because he is devoted to God and separated from the world, to whom must God be devoted for Him to be holy? The answer is that God's holiness means that God is entirely dedicated to being God. It is a supreme heresy to claim that there is any higher law or being than God. When identifying Himself in Exodus 3:14, He said, "I AM Who I AM." God is not holy because He follows someone else; no one is more supreme than God. God is not holy because He follows rules; He wrote the rules! God is not holy because He keeps the Law; His Law is what brings us closer to Him!

To say then that God is holy is to say God is God. "There is none holy like the Lord" (1 Sam. 2:2). "Holy, holy, holy is the Lord God Almighty, who was and is and is to come!" (Rev. 4:8). "To whom then will you compare Me, that I should be like him? says the Holy One" (Isa. 40:25). We cannot compare God to anyone. God is God alone, and thus God is holy.

> *To say that God is holy is to say God is God.*

Language is easily exhausted describing the holiness of God. We may call it greatness – majesty – power – awesomeness – perfection. But God's holiness is truly beyond words. We can only stand in silence as we stand before God in utter amazement. "The Lord is in His holy temple; let the earth keep silence before Him" (Hab. 2:20).

It is God's holiness that provides us with a pattern to imitate. "Let us cleanse ourselves from every defilement of body and spirit, bringing holiness to completion in the fear of God" (2 Cor. 7:1). We must "share in His holiness" (Heb. 12:10) and "strive [...] for the holiness without which no one will see the Lord" (Heb. 12:14). In Christ we are made holy (Eph. 5:27). There is nothing more important than to worship our holy God (1 Chron. 16:29). We long for the day for Christ to return; when all of creation will one day be entirely dedicated to the holiness of God (Zech. 14:20-21). Until then, we must be devoted to the sanctifying task of separating ourselves in God's service.

RIGHTEOUSNESS (JUSTICE)

Righteousness means *justice* and *rightness*. To say God is *righteous* is to say He is absolutely right and just and is the supreme standard for that which is right and just. When God acts, He always does what is right. With God, justice is inseparably connected to righteousness. He never punishes people more than the punishment they deserve, and He never forgets to reward those who deserve a reward. God is never unjust. It is impossible for God *not* to punish sin somehow (though punishment may not occur immediately), and it is impossible for God *not* to reward righteousness. If He fails to execute justice, He ceases to be God.

Note the Biblical basis for God's righteousness:

- **Because God is the just Judge, all of His judgments are perfectly in line with His righteousness.** "All His ways are justice. A God of faithfulness and without iniquity, just and upright is He" (Deut. 32:4).
- **God alone is our standard of morality and justice.** "There is no other god besides Me, a righteous God and a Savior; there is none besides Me" (Isa. 45:21). Abraham rhetorically asked God, "Shall not the Judge of all the earth do what is just?" (Gen. 18:25).
- **God is incapable of doing anything wrong.** "He does no injustice; every morning He shows forth His justice; each dawn He does not fail" (Zeph. 3:5).
- **God will be the final Judge.** "He has fixed a day on which He will judge the world in righteousness" (Acts 17:31). "He will render to each one according to his works" (Rom. 2:6).
- **God "judges impartially according to each one's deeds"** (1 Pet. 1:17). "His judgments are true and just" (Rev. 19:2).

People often get confused when they consider both God's

righteousness and God's grace, thinking that these attributes are mutually exclusive. If God must treat people as they deserve, why does He sometimes forgive people? Is this not a violation of God's very being? The answer to this question is found in the person of Jesus. God is able to forgive people because Christ died in order to receive God's punishment for Himself. The Apostle Paul explains the reason Christ was sacrificed on our behalf:

> This was to show God's righteousness, because in His divine forbearance He had passed over former sins. It was to show His righteousness at the present time, so that He might be just and the justifier of the one who has faith in Jesus. (Rom. 3:25-26)

The opposite of justice is injustice, which is evil. But mercy and grace are not opposed to justice – they are a sort of non-justice. It is not wrong for God to act mercifully; in fact, God's righteousness sometimes necessitates mercy. Both God's mercy and His righteousness are satisfied in Jesus Christ (Rom. 3:24-26). The Son of God *became* our sin (2 Cor. 5:21), so to speak, so we can find mercy and not have to endure eternal punishment.

And as children of God, we are required to act mercifully (Matt. 9:13). Justice is necessary to God's righteousness, but mercy and grace are optional. God is never required to be merciful, otherwise it would not be mercy – it would be entitlement. Justice is deserved, but mercy is voluntary.

We naturally find it repulsive when we see injustice in the world. That is because we are made in the image of God (Gen. 1:26-27). Thus, we should always pursue that which is right and seek justice for those who are not experiencing it. Proverbs 21:3 says, "To do righteousness and justice is more acceptable to the Lord than sacrifice."

JEALOUSY

We typically think of **jealousy** as a bad thing. If you were to conjure up in your imagination what you believed to be a perfect "God" (and thank the true God He isn't some sort of man-made invention), I doubt you would decide to make Him a *jealous* God. But plain as day, we find the true God repeatedly speaking of His jealousy throughout the Bible. He even names Himself "Jealous" (Ex. 34:14).

Note the Biblical basis for God's jealousy:

- **God described Himself as being jealous.** As God was explaining the commandments given to Moses on Mt. Sinai, He said, "I the Lord your God am a jealous God" (Ex. 20:5).
- **God has always been jealous for His people.** "Thus says the Lord of hosts: I am jealous for Zion with great jealousy, and I am jealous for her with great wrath" (Zech. 8:2).
- **God is jealous of anything that would replace Him as the object of man's worship.** "They stirred Him to jealousy with strange gods; with abominations they provoked Him to anger" (Deut. 32:16). "And Judah did what was evil in the sight of the Lord, and they provoked Him to jealousy with their sins that they committed, more than all that their fathers had done" (1 Kings 14:22).
- **Above all, God is jealous when we do not serve Him from the heart** (Jas. 4:5). "For they provoked Him to anger with their high places; they moved Him to jealousy with their idols" (Psa. 78:58). "Shall we provoke the Lord to jealousy? Are we stronger than He?" (1 Cor. 10:22).

How are we to make sense of this? We can understand God's jealousy on both a philosophical and a theological level.

THE PHILOSOPHICAL EXPLANATION OF GOD'S JEALOUSY

We understand that God is supreme and thus perfectly loving and holy. And whatever is perfectly and supremely loving and holy must be preserved and glorified with passionate zeal. It makes sense, then, that God's jealousy is His passionate zeal to preserve His holy supremacy. Therefore, God is justified in His jealousy (cf. Ex. 34:14).

THE THEOLOGICAL EXPLANATION OF GOD'S JEALOUSY

God's jealousy is His passionate zeal to preserve His holy supremacy.

The first theological explanation is that God's jealousy is an example of anthropomorphism. In other words, when the Bible describes God as being jealous, it is using familiar emotional imagery that we otherwise would not be able to understand. Just as the Bible is full of anthropomorphisms describing God in physical terms – e.g. God's hands, face, mouth, and eyes (cf. Ex. 7:5; Num. 6:25; Psa. 33:6; 34:15) – the Bible also uses anthropopathisms to describe God's emotions. While our own experiences of jealousy are often mixtures of spite, pride, envy, and weakness, there is no such thing with God. With God, His jealousy is a result of a holy hatred of evil and a zeal for that which is righteous and glorious.

The second theological explanation is that there are two kinds of jealousy. On one hand, **envy** is a kind of jealousy that is deeply wicked. It is expressed in the attitude, "I want what you have, and I hate you because you have what I do not have." Envy is the expression of covetousness. The wise man asks, "Wrath is cruel, anger is overwhelming, but who can stand before jealousy?" (Prov. 27:4). "Envy makes the bones rot" (Prov. 14:30). On the other hand, **zeal to protect a loving relationship** is a kind of righteous jealousy. A man who feels that his wife is unfaithful to him will feel this righteous sort of jealousy (cf. Num. 5:11-31). This, coupled with the desire to take vengeance on anything that destroys the loving relationship, is righteousness (cf. Prov. 6:34). God's jealousy is this second, righteous kind of jealousy.

In the above passages about God's jealousy, we understand that God demands absolute loyalty and devotion from those whom He loves. In His zealous jealousy, He has provided a way of salvation for all who would love and obey Him, and He hates sin and anything else that would threaten the loving relationship He has with His children. Above all, God must be glorified, and anything that diminishes God's glory will receive His furious recompense. God is "jealous for [His] holy name" (Eze. 39:25). "I am the Lord; that is my name; my glory I give to no other, nor my praise to carved idols" (Isa. 42:8; cf. 48:11).

WHAT GOD'S JEALOUSY MEANS TO THE CHRISTIAN

Because God is jealous for us, we are commanded to be jealous for Him. We must be "zealous for good works" (Titus 2:14) and zealous to repent (2 Cor. 7:11). Like Jesus, we must feel jealousy for the Lord when sin takes a hold of God's people (John 2:17).

Because Jesus is jealous for His church, His church should be jealous for Him. God hates the attitude of apathy and indifference among His people. Jesus said to the church in Laodicea,

> I know your works: you are neither cold nor hot. Would that you were either cold or hot! So, because you are lukewarm, and neither hot nor cold, I will spit you out of my mouth. (Rev. 3:15-16)

The Laodicea church of Christ lost its passionate zeal for Jesus, to which He responded: "be zealous and repent" (Rev. 3:19). How many churches today wear the name of Christ and are doctrinally sound, peaceful, respected – and *indifferent*? What would our jealous God say to them?

LOVE

One of the most misunderstood passages of the entire Bible is 1 John 4:8, where the Apostle John says, "God is love" (cf. v. 16). Many have divorced this verse from the rest of the Bible. "The only thing you need to know about God," one man said, "is that He is love." Is that so? And what *kind* of love is God, exactly? With this man's logic, why did the Biblical writers waste so many pages giving us the rest of the Bible, since "love" is supposedly the only thing you need to know about God?

We need the rest of the Bible to define God's love. Otherwise, we will be left with a false, little god who is soft, sentimental, whimsical, and indulgent. Those who hold this view will end up believing that

God will overlook many of the things He has forbidden. Another man said, "God will never send someone to hell because He is a God of love." Oh really? Was God the Son just joking about the eternal damnation of many (cf. Matt. 7:13-14; 25:41-46)? This man has failed to understand God's love in relation to God's holiness and justice.

When John said, "God is love," He was summing up the whole of what the Bible says about God. He assumed the reader would already be familiar with the rest of Scripture. The God John was speaking of is the same God who created the world, banished Adam from the garden and subjected the world to futility (Gen. 3:14-24; Rom. 8:20), destroyed the earth in a massive flood (Gen. 7:17-24), swallowed the family of Korah in the earth and consumed 250 men with fire (Num. 16:31-35), condemned an entire generation of Israelites to perish in the wilderness for forty years (Num. 14:26-38), sent His own Son to die on a cross to save humanity from sin, killed Ananias and Sapphira for misrepresenting their contribution to the church (Acts 5:1-11), and who will one day judge the whole world in righteousness. John says this God "is love."

GOD'S LOVE AS EXPLAINED BY HIS LIGHT AND SPIRIT NATURE

It is a perversion of the whole Bible to cite "God is love" in an effort to minimize God's hatred of sin and unfaithfulness. It may be helpful to understand "God is love" in conjunction with two other "God is" statements in the Bible, namely "God is spirit" (John 4:24) and "God is light" (1 John 1:5).

It is a perversion of the whole Bible to cite "God is love" in an effort to minimize God's hatred of sin and unfaithfulness.

"God is spirit" (John 4:24). Jesus uttered these words when He was teaching the Samaritan woman about acceptable worship. Because God is spirit, the *location* of our worship to Him does not matter; we can worship God in Samaria, in Jerusalem, in Tennessee, or in China. God is Spirit, and for

that matter He is omnipresent. Because God is spirit, He is not so
limited as we humans are in our fleshly bodies. Unlike us, with God
"there is no variation or shadow due to change" (Jas. 1:17). Also, as
a spirit, God is not inhibited by human passions such as fear, grief,
regret, lust, and desperation. Thus, God's love is not a fanciful, fickle,
fluctuating love like humans have. God loves just as a perfect, supreme,
immutable, spiritual God would love.

"God is light" (1 John 1:5). Evidently, many of the early Christians
in John's day, like many self-proclaimed Christians today, had come
to the harebrained conclusion that sin was "not a big deal." Many
today still believe that God's grace instantaneously forgives Christians
when they consciously violate God's Law. To which the Apostle Paul
responds, "Are we to continue in sin that grace may abound? By no
means! How can we who died to sin still live in it?" (Rom. 6:1-2).
Similarly, after saying "God is light," John continues, "in Him is no
darkness at all" (1 John 1:5).

> *At this time
> in 21ˢᵗ century
> America, "love"
> means accepting
> people **in** their sin,
> celebrating the
> diversity of sin,
> and never exposing
> sin. With God, love
> means delivering
> people **from** sin,
> celebrating those
> who are holy, and
> exposing darkness.*

"Light" refers to moral purity and
righteousness as defined by God's Law, and
"darkness" refers to sin and wickedness. Only
those who "walk in the light" (1 John 1:7) – the
light of God's holiness and righteousness – can
continue having fellowship with God. Those
who "walk in darkness" have been severed from
the love of God (cf. Jude 21).

The God who is love is both light and spirit.
Thus whatever sentimental ideas mankind has
about love is not God's love. In 21ˢᵗ century
America, "love" means accepting people *in* their
sin, celebrating the diversity of sin, and never
exposing sin. With God, love means delivering
people *from* sin, celebrating those who are holy,
and exposing darkness. And because God is
spirit, He does this impartially, consistently, and

perfectly. The Hebrews author writes,

> For the Lord disciplines the one He loves, and chastises every son
> whom He receives. [...] God is treating you as sons. For what son
> is there whom his father does not discipline? [...] He disciplines us
> for our good, that we may share in His holiness. For the moment all
> discipline seems painful rather than pleasant, but later it yields the
> peaceful fruit of righteousness to those who have been trained by it."
> (Heb. 12:6-11; cf. Prov. 3:12)

"God is love" (1 John 4:8, 16). What this means is that God is
eternally giving of Himself for the good of others. The Greek word
here for love is *agape*, referring to benevolent, self-sacrificing love.
Theologically, God's love refers to His **omnibenevolence**. God is
infinitely loving, making Him infinitely good. Jesus tells us that God's
love was active "before the foundation of the world" (John 17:24).
Who did God love before He created mankind? He loved the Son and
the Spirit (John 14:31; cf. 17:24).

Note the Biblical basis for God's love:

- **Jesus is the ultimate expression of God's love for mankind.**
  "In this is love, not that we have loved God but that He loved
  us and sent His Son to be the propitiation for our sins" (1 John
  4:10). "God shows His love for us in that while we were still
  sinners, Christ died for us" (Rom. 5:8).
- **God's love means He hates wrongdoing**. "For I the Lord love
  justice; I hate robbery and wrong" (Isa. 61:8).
- **God's love means He is faithful**. "I have loved you with an
  everlasting love; therefore I have continued my faithfulness to
  you" (Jer. 31:3).
- **God can experience sorrow due to a broken heart.** "And the
  Lord said to me, 'Go again, love a woman who is loved by
  another man and is an adulteress, even as the Lord loves the
  children of Israel, though they turn to other gods and love
  cakes of raisins" (Hosea 3:1).
- **Love is what motivated not only to create mankind, but also
  to save mankind.** "For God so loved the world, that He gave

His only Son, that whoever believes in Him should not perish but have eternal life" (John 3:16).

- ■ **No one (but ourselves) can sever the relationship we have with God.** "Who shall separate us from the love of Christ? Shall tribulation, or distress, or persecution, or famine, or nakedness, or danger, or sword? […] [Nothing] will be able to separate us from the love of God in Christ Jesus our Lord." (Rom. 8:35-39).

- ■ **God's love motivates us to action.** "For the love of Christ controls us, because we have concluded this: that one has died for all, therefore all have died" (2 Cor. 5:14).

- ■ **God's love should always motivate us to greater obedience and fear.** "See what kind of love the Father has given to us, that we should be called children of God" (1 John 3:1). "The Lord your God is in your midst, a mighty One who will save; He will rejoice over you with gladness; He will quiet you by His love; He will exult over you with loud singing" (Zeph. 3:17).

- ■ **And, after all of this, we would be remiss if we did not mention that great description of love in 1 Corinthians 13.**

Today, our relationship with God is based upon love. Jesus says, "If you love me, you will keep my commandments" (John 14:15). "Whoever has my commandments and keeps them, he it is who loves me. And he who loves me will be loved by my Father, and I will love him and manifest myself to him" (John 14:21). First and foremost, Jesus has commanded us to repent of our sins (Luke 13:3; cf. Acts 2:38), be baptized in His name for the remission of sins (Mark 16:15-16; Acts 22:16; 1 Pet. 3:21), and faithfully keep His commandments for the rest of life on earth (Rev. 2:10). That is how we show our love for Him, and that is how God demonstrates His love for us. Therefore, Paul can say, "If anyone has no love for the Lord, let him be accursed. Our Lord, come!" (1 Cor. 16:22).

GOODNESS

Jesus told the rich young ruler, "No one is good except God alone" (Luke 18:19). In other words, Jesus said, "Do not call me good unless you know me to be God, since only the Supreme God and Creator of the universe can truly be perfectly good." The goodness of God means He is the final and ultimate standard of good, and thus everything that God does is worthy of praise and approval. No one can achieve a higher level of goodness than God.

Note the Biblical basis for God's goodness:

- **The Psalms frequently say, "the Lord is good"** (Psa. 34:8; 100:5; 135:3; 145:9), or, "Oh give thanks to the Lord, for He is good" (Psa. 106:1; 107:1; 118:1, 29; 136:1).
- **When overwhelmed with His presence, humanity cannot help but exclaim God's goodness.** When fire came down from heaven and filled the temple with the glory of the Lord, in their awe the people of Israel worshipped God and exclaimed, "For He is good, for His steadfast love endures forever" (2 Chron. 7:3).
- **God is the ultimate source of everything that is good, since goodness is derived from God Himself.** "Every good gift and every perfect gift is from above, coming down from the Father of lights with whom there is no variation or shadow due to change" (Jas. 1:17).
- **God provides for those who are His.** "No good thing does He withhold from those who walk uprightly" (Psa. 84:11).
- **God will not overlook even the smallest of actions done on His behalf** (Matt. 10:42). Jesus reminds us that God will "give good things to those who ask Him" (Matt. 7:11).
- **Even God's discipline is ultimately the result of His deep goodness** (Heb. 12:10).

C.H. Spurgeon remarked,

> When others behave badly to us, it should only stir us up the more
> heartily to give thanks unto the Lord, because He is good; and when
> we ourselves are conscious that we are far from being good, we should
> only the more reverently bless Him that 'He is good.' We must never
> tolerate an instant's unbelief as to the goodness of the Lord; whatever
> else may be questionable, this is absolutely certain, that Jehovah is
> good; His dispensations may vary, but His nature is always the same,
> and always good.[3]

God's goodness manifests itself in two specific ways, namely *mercy*
and *grace*. Henry Thiessen summarizes these two avenues of God's
goodness: "Grace has respect to sinful man as guilty, while mercy has
respect to him as miserable and pitiful."[4] God told Moses, "And I will
be gracious to whom I will be gracious, and will show mercy on whom
I will show mercy" (Ex. 33:19; cf. Psa. 103:8; Heb. 4:16).

MERCY: GOD'S GOODNESS TOWARD THOSE IN MISERY AND DISTRESS

God's mercy is God's compassionate goodness toward those who are
suffering from the effects of sin. The psalmist pleaded with God, "Have
mercy on me, O God, according to your steadfast love; according to
your abundant mercy blot out my transgressions"
(Psa. 51:1). God's mercy is available to all
who seek Him. "For God has consigned all to
disobedience, that He may have mercy on all"
(Rom. 11:32; cf. 2 Pet. 3:9).

*God's goodness
manifests itself in
two specific
ways, namely
mercy and grace.*

GRACE: GOD'S GOODNESS TOWARD THOSE DESERVING PUNISHMENT

Always ask God for His grace; never ask God for justice – because you
might get it. Any sin – no matter how small – against an infinite God

---

3 C.H. Spurgeon, *The Treasury of David*, Vol. 5, p. 320
4 Henry Thiessen, *Lectures in Systematic Theology*, p. 87

logically deserves an infinite punishment. Since "all have sinned" (Rom. 3:23), all deserve eternal punishment. This is why we plead with God for His grace. God's grace is God's unmerited goodness toward sinners.

God has offered mankind salvation purely out of His good grace. Man does not deserve to be saved from his sins. Paul reminds us:

> For by grace you have been saved through faith. And this is not your own doing; it is the gift of God, not a result of works, so that no one may boast. (Eph. 2:8-9)

However, we must not overlook the fact that God's grace does not rule out man's obligation to faithfully obey Him. The Hebrews author says, "And being made perfect, [Jesus] became the source of eternal salvation to all who obey Him" (Heb. 5:9). God, in His perfect grace, offered mankind a way he can be saved.

WRATH

When was the last time you heard a sermon about God's wrath? Our secular culture has given itself up to the pursuit of money, pleasure, and convenience, and this pursuit has infiltrated the church. There are more and more churches who only want a steady drone of verbal cotton candy from their pulpits. Yet the writers of the Bible seem to be fixated on the wrath of God. Arthur Pink notes "a study of the concordance will show that there are more references in Scripture to the anger, fury, and wrath of God, than there are to His love and tenderness."[5]

Many believe that God's mercy and God's wrath are incompatible. On the contrary, it makes sense that a God who loves all that is good and righteous must also hate all sin. You cannot love one without hating the other. God's wrath burns hot toward anything that is opposed to His moral character, and He will eventually consume those who reject His Son and continue to live in sin.

We read John 3:36 where Jesus says, "Whoever does not obey the

---

5 Arthur Pink, *The Attributes of God*, p. 36

Son shall not see life, but the wrath of God remains on him." It is this "wrath of God," Paul says, that is "revealed from heaven against all ungodliness and unrighteousness of men" (Rom. 1:18). The Holy Spirit says that those who do not heed the words of the Lord "shall not enter [His] rest" (Heb. 3:11; cf. Rom. 2:5; 5:9; 9:22; Eph. 2:3; 1 Thess. 1:10; 2:16; 5:9; Heb. 10:31; 12:29; Rev. 6:16-17; 19:15). "Because God is holy," Pink continues, "He hates all sin; and because He hates all sin, His anger burns against the sinner (Psa. 7:11)."[6]

We should be thankful for God's wrath, because if God did not hate sin and unrighteousness, He would not be worthy of our utmost devotion and praise. And because God hates sin, His children must hate it too. We must follow Christ's example:

> You have loved righteousness and hated wickedness; therefore God, your God, has anointed you with the oil of gladness beyond your companions. (Heb. 1:9)

Because of God's grace, we are often not punished the moment we sin, and – when we become Christians – we have the peace of knowing we will not be punished for the rest of eternity.

We should not take pleasure in the downfall of others. Instead, we should pray that they would repent and obey the gospel of Christ before they experience God's wrath. We should, however, rejoice when justice is administered to evildoers. "When justice is done, it is a joy to the righteous" (Prov. 21:15). Those who have obeyed God's offer of salvation have satisfied God's wrath by means of the cross of Christ (cf. Rom. 3:25; 5:8-9).

We all deserve the wrath of God because of our sins (cf. Isa. 59:1-2). But those who have obeyed the gospel of Jesus Christ have no fear because the Son of God has atoned for our sins (Matt. 26:28; John 1:29; 1 John 2:2). Because of God's grace, we are often not punished the moment we sin, and – when we become Christians – we have the peace of knowing we will not be punished for

---

6 Ibid.

the rest of eternity. We must turn to Jesus and follow Him faithfully so we can flee the wrath that is to come (Matt. 3:7-8; 2 Thess. 1:7-9). "It is a fearful thing to fall into the hands of the living God" (Heb. 10:31).

CONCLUSION

A careful study of God's attributes tells us who He is and who He designed us to be. Without a doubt, the holiness, righteousness, jealousy, love, goodness, and wrath of God are perfect. As His children, let us pursue these qualities so we can better glorify our Father in heaven.

DISCUSSION QUESTIONS

1. In what ways can we be like God?

2. Why should we study God's attributes?

3. What is God's **jealousy**?

4. What is the difference between **envy** and **passionate zeal**?

5. What is God's **love**?

6. What two other "God is" passages help us better understand the phrase, "God is love" (1 John 4:8)?

7. How do we demonstrate our love for God?

8. What is God's **goodness**?

9. What is God's **wrath**?

10. How would you explain to someone that God's wrath and God's goodness are not opposed to one another?

CHAPTER 4

TWO'S COMPANY, THREE'S A CROWD, BUT THE LORD IS ONE

THE TRIUNE GODHEAD

IN the previous two chapters, we have discussed many of the attributes of God. But if we stopped now, we would not yet know the God of the Bible, for in His very being He has always existed as three Persons while still being one God. The tri-Personhood of God is one of the most difficult and mysterious of subjects to understand. And since the study of God is an infinite area of study, we can be sure that our finite minds will forever be unable to comprehend Him completely.

We often hear Christians say, "God is love." This is true, and entirely Biblical (1 John 4:8). Saying that God is love gives us warm feelings inside. After all, who doesn't want to serve a loving God? However, something that doesn't exactly roll off the tongue quite as easily is, "God is a Trinity." That just sounds stuffy and soggy with theology. But, while the doctrine of the Trinity might seem unimportant and weird – something that is just a curiosity to think about once in a while, we need to understand that God is love *because* He is a Trinity. But, more on that later.

The doctrine of the Trinity is central to Christianity, though sadly it is often neglected. To ignore the Trinity is to ignore the beautiful and satisfying answers to our deepest questions about God. When we strip God of His three-in-oneness, we end up forfeiting the God of the Bible. No matter how much we may have to mentally wrestle to better understand Him, *knowing God* is the heart of what it means to be a Christian. The more you come to know God, the more you will love Him (1 John 4:19). And when you gain a better understanding of the triune nature of God, you will inevitably become a better spouse, church member, and friend to those around you.

GETTING OUR TERMS RIGHT

There are two words that you should familiarize yourself with during this study: **Godhead** and **Trinity**. It is important that we use language that captures the essence of the triune nature of God so we can intelligently convey the powerful truths of the Bible to one another.

The term *Godhead* appears in the King James Version three times (Acts 17:29; Rom. 1:20; Col. 2:9) and the American Standard Version twice (Acts 17:29; Col. 2:9). In Acts 17:29, *Godhead* is translated from the Greek word *theion*, meaning "the deity." Here the apostle Paul is using *theion* to teach the Greek people about the only true God as opposed to their false gods. In Romans 1:20, *Godhead* is translated from the Greek word *theiotés*, meaning "divine nature" or "divine essence." Paul uses *theiotés* to teach that even unbelievers can learn about the divine nature of God by studying creation. In Colossians 2:9, *Godhead* is translated from the Greek word *theotés*, meaning "deity." Paul applies *theotés* to Jesus in one of the most emphatic affirmations of the deity of Christ.

In all three of these passages, *Godhead* really just means an all-encompassing "Godhood," which basically refers to that which makes God, God. Today, however, the meaning of *Godhead* has changed and has come to express more specifically the divine essence shared by all three divine personalities:[1] Father, Son, and Holy Spirit (e.g. Matt 28:19; 1 Cor. 12:4-6; 2 Cor. 13:14; Eph. 4:4-6; 1 Pet. 1:2; Jude 20-21). In contemporary times, when we say *Godhead*, we often use it synonymously with **Trinity**.

The word *Trinity* is not found in the Bible, but the idea it represents

---

1 Wayne Jackson, "What About the Terms 'Godhead' and 'Trinity'?"

is affirmed throughout the pages of Scripture. *Trinity* is a perfectly legitimate word used to describe what is undoubtedly revealed to us in God's Word. We must, however, allow Scripture to define our doctrine of the *Trinity*, instead of projecting an extra-biblical understanding onto the Bible. Never should we go beyond Scripture in our attempt to understand the *Trinity*, as is often done in Christendom today.[2]

Trinity just means "tri-unity," and is derived from the Latin word *trinas*, meaning "threefold." Implied in the concept of "unity" is **monotheism**, which is the Biblical affirmation that there is one God. In short, *Trinity* means there is one God in three Persons. The three Persons of the Godhead are distinct Persons yet fully God in essence and nature.

It is likely that we find an allusion to the three Persons of the Godhead in the angelic choir in Isaiah 6:3 and later in Revelation 4:8 as they stood before the throne of God, proclaiming, "Holy, holy, holy!"[3] Because this Biblical scene is so potent, Christians often sing the words of that great hymn:

> Holy, Holy, Holy, Lord God Almighty!
> Early in the morning our song shall rise to Thee;
> Holy, Holy, Holy! Merciful and Mighty!
> God in Three persons, blessed Trinity![4]

NOT JUST STRANGER THAN FICTION

Many have turned the Trinity into a mere oddity – something obscure and, at times, downright bizarre. The way church members sometimes talk about the Trinity (if they dare to approach the subject in the first place) unintentionally reinforces a sort of stigma about the Godhead. One well-meaning person may say, "We should think of the Trinity like an egg; there are three parts – yolk, shell, and white – but together

---

2 John Thompson, *Modern Trinitarian Perspectives*, p. 4
3 Actually, in some ancient manuscripts of Isaiah 6:3 and Revelation 4:8 we find "Holy, holy, holy!" expressed in three sets of three, literally "Holy, holy, holy, Holy, holy, holy, Holy, holy, holy!"
4 Sadly, editors of several of today's popular hymn books have taken the liberty of changing the original Trinitarian wording of the song *Holy, Holy, Holy* to, "God over all, and blest eternally." We are not sure why they did this, and we think this alteration is regretable.

they comprise one egg." "No," another might say, "the Trinity is like a three-leaf clover – three leaves, one plant." And another inventive person chimes in (and I've actually heard this one too), "You both have it wrong. The Trinity is like 3-in-1 shampoo – three products, one substance."

And we wonder why the secular world often laughs at Christians. When we claim the Trinity is "just like" an egg, H_2O, plant, shampoo, Neapolitan ice cream, business committee, apple, or three-headed monster, we make God sound kind of... well, freaky – like old uncle Ned's giant mole that he taunts his little nieces and nephews with during every family Thanksgiving gathering. When the Trinity is merely seen as a sort of blob to be poked at, no wonder the church has avoided the subject. The shampooishness of God can never be anything more to people than a mere weird, curious novelty.

While simple analogies sometimes help us understand spiritual truths, they often do more harm than good when applied to the Trinity. Comparing God to the three leaves of a clover or the three parts of an egg is dangerous because each part is not fully the clover or egg, but each member of the Godhead is fully God. Comparing God to the three forms of water is dangerous because no individual quantity of water can't be all three forms at the same time, though God is simultaneously the Father, the Son, and the Holy Spirit. No illustration captures the essential relationship between the loving eternal Father and the obedient eternal Son. All human analogies fail to capture the full essence of God and end up suggesting either the false doctrines of *modalism*, *Arianism*, or *tritheism*. (Don't worry – we go into greater details about these later in the chapter.)

Without a doubt, the Trinity is an enigma – much like the question, "Who made God?" No one made God; He has always been. Try wrapping your mind around God's eternality. Likewise, God is both one and three, and thankfully we do not have to fully grasp that concept before we can accept it. We will never be able to neatly package God into a comfortable box. We simply must believe in the

Trinity because the concept is so unavoidably taught in the Bible. The only word that fully describes the logistics of the three Persons of the Godhead is the word "mystery." Moses reminds us, "The secret things belong to the Lord" (Deut. 29:29). But much like God has revealed the mystery of salvation to the entire world (cf. Eph. 3:2-6), God has revealed some of the facts of the mystery of Himself to us: He is one God, and He is Father, Son, and Holy Spirit. But an element of mystery will always remain.

Even though it is an enigma to us, the Trinity is not a problem. By studying the three Persons of God as revealed in Scripture, we can better know, serve, and love God in His glory.

A SUMMARY OF WHAT THE BIBLE TEACHES ABOUT THE TRIUNE GODHEAD

THERE IS ONE GOD

We do not serve three Gods; the God of the Bible is only one Being. This is taught throughout the Bible, and perhaps the most well-known passage is Deuteronomy 6:4: "Hear, O Israel: The Lord our God, the Lord is one." This is followed by the familiar words, "You shall love the Lord your God with all your heart and with all your soul and with all your might" (v. 5). Jesus later quoted this verse, saying, "Hear, O Israel: The Lord our God, the Lord is one" (Mark 12:29). Jesus was a **monotheist**.[5]

When God speaks, He repeatedly says that He is the only true God. This is significant because, in the ancient world, God's people were usually surrounded by *polytheistic* cultures. **Polytheism** is the belief that there is a plurality of gods, and thus thoroughly opposed to the teaching of Scripture. It would have been much easier for the prophetic authors of the Bible to speak of God as three Gods. Instead, time and time again, the Bible affirms that God alone is the only true God, and

---

5 Monotheism is the belief that there is only one God.

there is none like Him. And when God speaks, He does not speak of Himself as one among three whom we are to worship. Instead, God says:

> I am the Lord, and there is no other,
>   besides me there is no God;
> I equip you, though you do not know me,
>   that people may know, from the rising of the sun
>   and from the west, that there is none besides me;
> I am the Lord, and there is no other. (Isa. 45:5-6)

Throughout the Bible we find the emphatic declaration that we serve only one God. "Let these words of mine […] be near to the Lord our God […], that all the peoples of the earth may know that the Lord is God; there is no other" (1 Kings 8:59-60). "I am God, and there is no other; I am God, and there is none like me" (Isa. 46:9). "And this is eternal life, that they know you the only true God" (John 17:3). "God is one" (Rom. 3:30). "There is one God" (1 Cor. 8:6). "For there is one God" (1 Tim. 2:5). "You believe that God is one; you do well. Even the demons believe – and shudder!" (Jas. 2:19). Other examples could be cited. (See also 2 Sam. 7:22; 2 Kings 19:15; 1 Chron. 17:20; Neh. 9:6; Jer. 23:23-24; Psa. 83:18; 86:10; Isa. 40:28; 43:10-11; 57:15.)

In today's age of **pluralism**,[6] these texts are enormously relevant. There is only one God, and He reigns over all people. All men must bow before Him, or they will perish.

GOD IS THREE PERSONS

There can be no doubt that we serve only one God. But we do not get off quite so easily – the Bible just as plainly teaches that God is a unity of three distinct Persons. For instance, in Genesis 1:26, God said, "Let *us* make man in *our* image, after *our* likeness." To whom was God talking? He was not talking to angels, because man is not made in the image of angels, but "in the image of God" (Gen. 1:27). God used the

---

6 Pluralism is the belief that there are many equally valid ethical systems and religions. America is an increasingly pluralistic society. Those who hold to pluralism believe that religions like Buddhism, Islam, Christianity, and Judaism are equal, and no single religion is more "right" than the other.

words "us" and "our," implying that more than one divine Person was involved in creation.

The Son is not the Father. In John 1:1-2, we read, "In the beginning was the Word, and the Word was with God, and the Word was God." The Word – another name for Jesus Christ (cf. v. 9-18) – was "with" God, demonstrating a distinction between the Father and the Son. We also find that Jesus, the Son of God, now serves as our advocate and High Priest before God the Father. "We have an advocate with the Father, Jesus Christ the righteous" (1 John 2:1; cf. Heb. 7:25). To serve in this capacity, Jesus the Son of God must be a separate Person from the Father. Furthermore, Jesus said the Father sent Him (John 5:23, 36) and that He was going back to the Father (John 14:12); He said He came not to do His Will but the Father's Will (John 4:34; 6:38); He said His Father gave Him His sheep (John 6:39; 10:29). Clearly, the Father and the Son are not the same Person.

The Holy Spirit is not the Father. Jesus told His disciples: "When the Helper comes, whom I will send to you from the Father, the Spirit of truth, who proceeds from the Father, He will bear witness about me" (John 15:26; cf. 14:26, 16:13). In addition to being sent by the Father to communicate the revelation of Jesus (cf. Rev. 2:11), the Holy Spirit also "intercedes" for Christians before the Father (Rom. 8:27).

The Holy Spirit is not the Son. We find this implied in Trinitarian[7] passages such as Matthew 28:19 and 2 Corinthians 13:14. We also know this due to the fact that when Jesus ascended back to heaven, He sent the Holy Spirit to reveal His Word to the church. Jesus said, "It is to your advantage that I go away, for if I do not go away, the Helper will not come to you. But if I go, I will send Him to you" (John 16:7).

When we say that God is three Persons, we mean that the Father is not the Son, the Father is not the Holy Spirit, and the Holy Spirit is not the Son; they are all distinct from one another. This boggles the mind. Even now, as I type, "God is three Persons," my computer's

---

7 That is, a passage which alludes to the Trinity

word processor is underlining the phrase with squiggly lines, thinking it is incorrect grammar. Do not think of the Persons of the Godhead as you would *created* human beings, with bodies made out of skin and bones. Instead, as Jack Cottrell proposes, think of God this way: "That God is three Persons means that within the one divine nature are three individual centers of consciousness."[8]

> *That God is three Persons means that within the one divine nature are three individual centers of consciousness.*

God has eternally existed as three Persons – Father, Son, and Holy Spirit – and each one is fully God, and there is only one God in essence. Though this is a mystery, it is not a contradiction. It would only be a contradiction if God were both three *and* one Persons at the same time. No, God is three Persons in *one essence.*[9] And we must make this distinction between the Persons of the Godhead because the Bible makes this distinction. We must accept this if we are to be "people of the Book."

EACH PERSON OF THE GODHEAD IS FULLY GOD

Roy Lanier Jr. writes, "In careful reading of the Scriptures, one is forced to conclude there are three distinctions to be made in studying about God, all of whom are called 'God.'"[10]

First, God the Father is God. "…For us there is one God, the Father, from whom are all things…" (1 Cor. 8:6). The apostle Paul began his Galatian letter with, "Paul, an apostle—not from men nor through man, but through Jesus Christ and God the Father…" (Gal. 1:1). John said, "on [Jesus] God the Father has set His seal…" (John 6:27). Jesus prayed, "I thank you, Father, Lord of heaven and earth…" (Matt. 11:25). (See also Mark 14:36; John 4:23-24; 11:41; 17:11; 20:17; Phil. 2:11.)

---

8 Jack Cottrell, *The Faith Once for All*, p. 71
9 By "essence" we mean the essential properties/attributes of God. For example, God is in essence a *spirit*; God is in essence *loving*; God is in essence *righteous*. Likewise, God is in essence *one*.
10 Roy Lanier Jr., *What Do You Know About God?*, p. 133

Second, God the Son is God. John 1:1-18 could not teach any more plainly that Christ is God. In that passage, Jesus, called "the Word," and is seen as both "God" and "with God." You may also recall when the apostle Thomas doubted whether Jesus had been raised from the dead, saying he would not believe in Jesus unless he first saw the nail prints in Jesus' hands and could place his hand into Jesus' side (John 20:25). Eight days later, when Jesus appeared again to the apostles, Thomas exclaimed, "My Lord and my God!" (John 20:28), and both Jesus and the apostle John (who penned the gospel of John) approved of Thomas' words (John 20:29-31).

During Jesus' earthly ministry, He taught, "I and the Father are One." His audience took this to mean that He was referring to Himself as God (John 10:30-33). The apostle Paul wrote that he was "waiting for our blessed hope, the appearing of the glory of our great God and Savior Jesus Christ" (Titus 2:13). And as cited earlier, Paul said, "In Him the whole fullness of deity dwells bodily" (Col. 2:9). (See also Rom. 9:5; Phil. 2:6; Heb. 1:8; 1 John 5:20.)

Third, God the Spirit is God. When Ananias lied to the Holy Spirit, Peter said, "You have not lied to man but to God" (Acts 5:3-4). The Holy Spirit is placed at an equal level with God the Father and God the Son (Matt. 28:19). Only the Spirit of God knows the thoughts of God (1 Cor. 2:11-12), and who can know the thoughts of God except God Himself? The Holy Spirit is so important that disbelieving in His witness is a blasphemy that cannot be forgiven (Matt. 12:31-33). Knowing that the temple of God is where God dwells, Paul said the temple is where God's Spirit is found (1 Cor. 3:16). Christ was offered to God through the "eternal Spirit" (Heb. 9:14). (See also Rom. 8:9-11; 2 Cor. 3:17-18; 13:14; Eph. 4:4-6; 1 Pet. 1:2; Jude 20-21.)

The Father, Son, and Holy Spirit are not one-third God each. Instead, each is God and subsists under the presence of deity.

Each person of the Godhead is fully God. The Father, Son, and Holy Spirit are not 1/3 God each. Instead, each is fully God and subsists under the presence of deity. So what exactly distinguishes each Person of the Godhead? It cannot be His nature, for by His nature each is equal as God. What distinguishes each is His role and relationship. To better understand the Godhead, we must discern the individual roles and relationships of each Person as expressed in Scripture.

WHO IS GOD?

WHAT WAS GOD DOING BEFORE HE CREATED THE WORLD?

What one description best captures the essence of the God of the Bible? It can't be "Creator," because there was a time when there was no creation. Of course, God is certainly the Creator, but if God's identity were first and foremost the "Creator," then He would need a creation to rule over in order to be God. This would mean God somehow *needs* us. The God of the Bible also surely can't be reduced to "Ruler," though God is most certainly the Ruler of the Universe. If "Ruler" were His only identity, salvation would be limited to mere forgiveness for breaking His rules (instead of eternity in His loving presence). He also can't be reduced to "Almighty," though God is certainly the Almighty. Yet God is more than just a pure, unlimited, powerful force.

I believe we find our answer in the Son of God. Jesus said, "Whoever has seen Me has seen the Father" (John 14:9). Jesus is our key to understanding God. The fact that Christ is known as "the Son" (cf. John 3:35) means He has a Father. God the Son shows us principally – above all other words we could use to describe Him – that God is a Father. "I am the way, the truth, and the life. No one comes to the Father except through Me" (John 14:6). More than "Creator," "Ruler," or "Almighty," God has revealed Himself to be a Father.

One of the most insightful texts in helping us understand the

Trinity is John 17:24, where Jesus prayed, "Father, […] you loved me before the foundation of the world." What was God doing before He created the world? God the Father was loving the Son.

The chief image of God in the Bible is that of a **Father** (cf. Ex. 4:22; Isa. 1:2; 63:16; 64:8; Jer. 3:4; 31:9; Hos. 11:1; Deut. 1:31; 8:5; 32:6; Psa. 103:13; Jer. 3:4, 19; Mal. 1:6; John 20:17; Rom. 15:6; 1 Cor. 1:3; 8:6; Heb. 12:7; 1 Pet. 1:3). He is this at the core of His being. He creates and gives life like a Father, He rules as a Father, He exercises His power as a Father. And only when we realize that God rules and creates as a Father can we begin to delight in His Law and His providence.

THE FATHER LOVES THE SON

The apostle John writes,

> Anyone who does not love does not know God, because God is love. In this the love of God was made manifest among us, that God sent His only Son into the world, so that we might live through Him. (1 John 4:8-9)

God could not be love if there was at any point no one to love. Without a Son, God could not be a Father. Yet God did not have to (nor did He) create the Son in order to be who He is. Again, Jesus said in John 17:24, "You loved me before the foundation of the world." Jesus, who is "before all things" (Col. 1:17) is the eternal Son. Through the Son "all things were created" (Col. 1:16) and by Him "all the foundations of the earth" were laid (Heb. 1:10).

The Father's identity is seen through His love for the Son. This is why it is vitally important that we know that the Son is eternal just as the Father is eternal. There was never a time in which He didn't exist; otherwise, God would not be the Father and God could not be love (because there must always be a recipient of love for there to be love). The Son is the very image of God. Thus Hebrews 1:3 says, "He is the radiance of the glory of God and the exact imprint of His nature, and

He upholds the universe by the word of His power." C.S. Lewis wrote,

> The words 'God is love' have no real meaning unless God contains at
> least two Persons. Love is something that one person has for another
> person. If God was a single Person, then before the world was made,
> He was not love.[11]

Roy Lanier Sr. wrote,

> In order for [God] to have the eternal attribute of love, there had to
> be an object for Him to love. Objects of the Father's love are found in
> the Son and the Holy Spirit.[12]

THE FUNCTIONAL ORDER OF THE TRINITY

Love best explains the paradox of the Trinity. The Father loves the
Son (John 3:35; 5:20). The Son loves the Father (John 14:31). In fact,
the Son so loves the Father that He is submissive to Him in all things
(John 4:34; 6:38).

This is very significant because 1 Corinthians 11:3 says, "I want you
to understand that the head of every man is Christ, the head of a wife
is her husband, and the head of Christ is God." In some mysterious
way, there is a sort of hierarchy in the Godhead – not in importance
(no Person of the Godhead is more *God* than the other), but in role.
The Father loves the Son and is His head, and the Son loves the
church. "As the Father has loved me, so I have loved you" (John 15:9).
And thus "we love because He first loved us" (1 John 4:19). As a result,
the Father's love for the Son is the model for how husbands are to love
their wives (Eph. 5:25). A man must first and foremost love his wife
freely, not primarily because she respects him, but because Christ first
and foremost loves the church (Eph. 5:22-25).

We must stress that all members of the Trinity are equal in
essence, but they have different roles. This is often called **functional
subordination**. First, there is the Father, and by this very title we

---

11   C.S. Lewis, *Beyond Personality*, p. 21
12   Roy Lanier Sr., *The Timeless Trinity*, p. 58

find His functional precedence to that of the Son and the Holy Spirit. Throughout the Bible, we see the Father as the sender and the planner of salvation. Second, there is the Son, and by this title we find submission to the Father. The Father sent, and the Son came to us; the Father planned our salvation, and the Son accomplished our salvation. The Bible depicts the Son as from the Father, but nowhere is the Father said to be from the Son. Third, there is the Holy Spirit, who proceeds from both the Father and the Son (John 15:26).

THE ROLE OF THE SPIRIT

At the baptism of Jesus we find all three members of the Godhead present:

> When Jesus also had been baptized and was praying, the heavens were opened, and the Holy Spirit descended on Him in bodily form, like a dove; and a voice came from heaven, "You are my beloved Son; with you I am well pleased." (Luke 3:21-22)

Here we find the Son, the Father, and the Holy Spirit. And by giving the Son the Holy Spirit, the Father demonstrates His love for the Son. The scene is reminiscent of the scene of creation, when "the Spirit of God was hovering over the face of the waters" (Gen. 1:2). As the Spirit was present at the creation of the world, the Spirit was present at the inaugural event of Jesus' ministry. God creates by His Word (who would later go on to become flesh and dwell among us, John 1:14), and He does so by sending His Word by the power of the Spirit. It is by the Spirit that the Father empowers the Son (cf. Luke 10:21), and it is by means of the Spirit that we come to know about the love of God (2 Pet. 1:20-21).

FALSE VIEWS OF THE TRINITY

MODALISM

Modalism is the doctrine that the Father, the Son, and the Holy Spirit are all the same Person. Those who hold to this view claim that the Father, the Son, and the Holy Spirit are simply different "modes" or "forms" in which God decides to manifest Himself. It goes something like this: In the Old Testament, God appeared mostly in the form of a "Father," then throughout the Gospel accounts as a "Son." After the ascension of Christ, God took the form of the Holy Spirit.

Among many reasons why *modalism* is false, the biggest problem is the obvious relationship each member of the Godhead has with the others. For example, *modalism* must deny that all three Persons of the Godhead were present during the baptism of Jesus, where the Spirit of God "descended like a dove" to "rest on Him" and the Father spoke from heaven, saying, "This is My beloved Son, with whom I am well pleased" (Matt. 3:16-17; Luke 3:21-22). As another example, *modalism* must reduce all the instances of Jesus praying to the Father to a mere illusion (cf. cf. Matt. 11:25-26, Luke 10:21; John 11:41-42; 12:27-28; 17:1-26; Matt. 26:36-44, Mark 14:32-39, Luke 22:42; Matt. 27:46, Mark 15:34, Luke 23:34, 46). As yet another example, *modalism* severely weakens the idea of the Holy Spirit interceding on our behalf before the Father (Rom. 8:26). This is why using H_2O as an illustration of God is so dangerous, because a single measurement of water cannot be both ice, liquid, and gas at the same time.

Modalism is the view of the **United Pentecostal Church**, and adherents of this church are sometimes known as "Oneness Pentecostals." Because they deny the triune nature of God taught so explicitly in Scripture, this religious group is actually not a "Christian" group at all.

ARIANISM

Arianism is named after Arius, who lived in the 4th century and taught that at some point God the Father created God the Son, and that before that time God the Son and God the Holy Spirit did not exist. *The Watchtower Society/Jehovah's Witness Sect*, which believes Jesus is just a created being and that the Holy Spirit is essentially just the inanimate power of God, is a modern-day example of *Arianism*. Because it denies the deity of Christ, *Arianism* also rejects the Biblical truth that the Son of God completely atoned for our sins (cf. Isa. 53:11). *Arians* and *Jehovah's Witnesses* are far from being Christians, as they completely deny the deity of Christ.

TRITHEISM

Tritheism is a form of *polytheism*, and is the doctrine that there are actually three Gods. *Tritheists* believe the Father, Son, and Holy Spirit do not share the same essence, and – while they may be united in purpose – they are individually distinct from one another. This is why the "committee" illustration of the Trinity is dangerous, because it reinforces the idea that the Godhead is actually comprised of three Gods. Passages like Isaiah 45:5 and John 5:44 refute *tritheism*.

Mormonism is a hybrid form of *tritheism*, as Mormons deny that there is only one God. More specifically, *Mormonism* teaches that many gods exist, though they teach we are to worship only God the Father. According to Mormonism, the godhead over the earth is compromised of three separate gods: the Father, the Son, and the "Holy Ghost," with the Father and Son having bodies of flesh and bone.[13] The Father used to be a man on another world who happened to bring one of his wives to this world, where they conceived several sons, including the Son,[14] the "Holy Ghost," and Lucifer (the devil). Therefore, *Mormonism* is technically *polytheistic*, but with a *tritheistic* "spin."

Religious groups that actually believe *tritheism* are rare today, but Christians can unintentionally develop tritheistic views toward the Trinity by forgetting that the Father, the Son, and the Holy Spirit are one God and share the same divine essence. For example, the vocal minority of Christians who strongly believe it is wrong to worship the Son or the Holy Spirit need to be deeply careful that they do not argue their position on the basis that the Son and the Spirit are somehow

---

13 *Doctrine & Covenants* 130:22
14 Alma 36:17

different in essence from the Father. God cannot be separated; He is one. The Son and the Spirit are as much God as the Father is God. Our triune God, *Yahweh*, is worthy of worship (Psa. 18:3), and He is the Father, Son, and Holy Spirit – united in essence and distinct only in personality.

Another example of how easy it is for Christians to develop a *tritheistic* view towards the Trinity is the idea that the Holy Spirit dwells within Christians in a different manner or more literal way than the Son or the Father dwells within Christians. Roy Lanier Sr. correctly observes,

> If we say, as some are wont to affirm, that Jesus is not on earth, He is in heaven, and the Holy Spirit was sent to earth, we separate the Persons of the Godhead so as to become *tritheistic* in the use of these terms.[15] (emp. added)

We must remember that all Persons of the Godhead, as God, are omnipresent. Where one is, the other is (cf. 2 Cor. 3:17-18). The Lord promised His apostles that He would be with them when the Spirit comes to them (John 14:18; cf. Matt. 28:20). Both the Father and the Son dwell within the heart of the Christian in the same representative manner as the Spirit does (Eph. 3:17; Col. 1:27; 2 Cor. 6:16; Rom. 8:9-11).

FEMINISM/EGALITARIANISM

Do not be so naïve to think that modern **feminism** is merely the belief that women are equal to men in value. If this were the extent of what feminists believed, they would be right. The Bible teaches that men and women do in fact have equal worth (Gal. 3:26-29). But modern *feminism* goes way too far in arguing that men and women must have equal roles, too. This is called **egalitarianism**, which is the belief that there should be no gender distinctions in the church and in the home.

Modern feminists find what the Bible teaches about submission

---

15 Roy Lanier Sr., *The Timeless Trinity*, p. 55

to be offensive, falsely equating "submission" with "inequality." Yet the principle of submission is vitally important for all Christians. The wife is equal to her husband *in value* but is to be submissive to her husband *in her role* (1 Cor. 11:3; Eph. 5:22-23). Christians are equal in value to one another yet they are taught to "submit to one another out of reverence for Christ" (Eph. 5:21). Christ was submissive to Pontius Pilate, though no one can argue that He was somehow inferior to Pilate (Matt. 27:11-14). Citizens are to be submissive to their government (Rom. 13:1-7) and Christians are to be submissive to the leaders of the church (Heb. 13:17), otherwise there would be anarchy.

Equally important is the fact that Christ is equal to God the Father and yet was subject to Him (Phil. 2:6-8). The logic of feminism, however, is a great insult to the Trinity. Scripture affirms that the Father, Son, and Holy Spirit are equal in being and personhood (cf. John 1:1; 5:23; 10:30; 14:6-7, 9, 11) yet they hold different roles or functions. The Son voluntarily is subject and subordinate to the Father (John 5:19-20; 6:38; 8:28-29, 54; 1 Cor. 15:28; Phil. 2:5-11), and the Holy Spirit is under the direction of the Father and is sent by Him to glorify the Son (John 14:26; 15:26; 16:13-14). Are you ready to assign inferiority to the Son and the Holy Spirit the way egalitarians assign inferiority to role submission in the home and in the church?

Some feminists are bold enough to say we should strip God of any masculine terminology by claiming words like "Father," "Son," "He," "Him," and "His" are oppressive to women. One feminist argues,

> Masculine terms such as Father or Son are heard as referring to males. The constant use of such terms and the absence of comparable female terms increases exclusivity according to gender in church and society.[16]

However, the stubborn fact is that the Bible *never* uses feminine language to name God. It is true that God does not have an actual gender, and it is also true that sometimes God is sometimes described with feminine imagery (cf. Isa. 42:14; 46:3; 49:15; Matt. 23:37). But God is never called "Mother" and Christ is never

---

16 Susan Thistlethwaite, "On The Trinity"

called "Daughter." We must respect how God has chosen to reveal Himself in Scripture. One author observed, "The names for God – Yahweh, Elohim, Shaddai, Sebbaoth, Adonai, Kurios, and Theos — are all masculine gender."[17] To ignore how God describes Himself is to irreparably distort the relationship the Father, the Son, and the Holy Spirit have with one another.

CALVINISM

You may ask, "What does **Calvinism**[18] have to do with the Trinity?" Calvinism is built entirely on a false definition of God's sovereignty,[19] defining "sovereignty" as "absolute use of absolute power and absolute control at absolutely all times."[20] This definition of God's sovereignty is not only unnecessary, it is also unbiblical (see chapter 6). Yet Calvinists reject the fact that God allows everyone the freedom to choose whether or not to obey the gospel from the heart and be saved (cf. Rom. 6:17). Instead, as one Calvinist argues, "God is in the back of everything. He decides and causes all things to happen that do happen."[21] Calvinists believe that the idea that God could ever be submissive to another person's will is preposterous. In the words of another famous (yet mistaken) Calvinist, John Piper, "non-omnipotent

> *Calvinism's definition of God's sovereignty is incompatible with the fact that God the Son is submissive to the Father.*

---

17 Bert Thompson, "Is God Male?"
18 **Calvinism**, also known as Reformed theology, is basically the body of religious teaching started by John Calvin (1509 – 1564 A.D.) and other Reformation-era theologians such as Ulrich Zwingli and Jonathan Edwards. Calvinism began fundamentally as a response to the false teaching that man must *work* his way to heaven by performing good deeds and somehow meriting his salvation (which is to say that God *owes* good men and women salvation). Calvinism correctly points out the error of this teaching, reminding us of Paul's teaching that *justification* can only happen by God's grace, and the way we come in contact with God's grace is through faith (not through works so that none of us may boast, cf. Eph. 2:8-9). However, **Calvinism goes much too far** by claiming that because justification and salvation are *exclusively* from God, man must have absolutely *nothing* to do with his salvation. Calvinism teaches that because man cannot contribute anything to his salvation it must be because man is inherently evil and therefore has nothing to contribute but darkness. This is the Calvinistic teaching of Total depravity. With man totally depraved and unable to contribute anything to his salvation, it is up to God to select (elect) individuals randomly to save without requiring them to do anything to be saved. This is the Calvinistic teaching of Unconditional election. If no man can choose to be saved — and it is exclusively God's prerogative which individuals He will respect enough to save — then it logically follows that Christ's atoning work on the cross was exclusively for the elect and no one else. This is the Calvinistic teaching of Limited atonement. If you are among the few that God has arbitrarily chosen to be saved, you then are unable to refuse His destiny for you. This is the Calvinistic teaching of Irresistible grace. Therefore, since man cannot do anything for his salvation, there is nothing he can do to *lose* his salvation if he was selected by God to be saved. Hence, once the elect are saved, they can never lose their salvation. This is the Calvinistic teaching of Perseverance of the saints. We praise God, however, that Calvinism is wrong and that mankind does have a choice in his salvation. For a greater discussion on Calvinism, go to page 86.
19 F. LaGard Smith, *Troubling Questions for Calvinists,* p. 21
20 Austin Fischer, *Young, Restless, No Longer Reformed,* p. 68
21 Edwin H. Palmer, *The Five Points of Calvinism,* p. 25

omnipotence is a self-contradiction."[22] Piper believes that for God to allow another person's will to happen in a way that somehow brings God disappointment somehow strips God of His omnipotence. In summary, Calvinism asserts that God, because He is God, cannot possibly submit Himself to anyone.

Again, "What does this have to do with the Trinity?" Calvinism's definition of God's sovereignty is incompatible with the fact that God the Son is submissive to the Father. However, the Bible teaches that God the Son is sovereign over all (Matt. 28:18). And, as sovereign God, He made Himself submissive to God the Father (John 6:38; 14:28; 20:17; Acts 4:27, 30; 1 Cor. 11:3; 2 Cor. 1:3; Heb. 10:5-7; et. al.). How can Calvinism explain the submission of God the Son to God the Father without stripping the Son of His deity? It can't. Obviously, just as God in His sovereignty can choose to give mankind a degree of free choice, God the Son in His sovereignty can choose to be submissive to the Father.

WHY THE DOCTRINE OF THE TRINITY IS VITALLY IMPORTANT

The fact that God is a Trinity should be a precious truth to us, every bit as worthy of being defended as any other important doctrine of Scripture. Here's why:

First, without the Trinity, there is no hope of being reconciled with God. Our sins have separated us from the eternal God (Isa. 59:1-2). Only infinite God could bear the price of sin against infinite God. Therefore, if Jesus is not God, then how could He bear the full wrath of God against our sins (cf. Heb. 5:8-9)? Roy Lanier Sr., wrote,

> One Person of the Godhead became the God-man, and now there is one God and one mediator between God and man, Himself man, Christ Jesus (1 Tim. 2:5). If God were not three Persons in one essence, this mediatorship would have been impossible, so no

---

22 John Piper, *The Pleasures Of God*, p. 58

redemption for man.[23]

Second, without the Trinity, we cannot have confidence in our salvation. If Jesus is not God, how can we trust Him to bear our salvation, since He would merely be a created being? We pity Jehovah's Witnesses, who believe the heretical teaching that the Son of God is just a creature. In reality, Jesus the Son of God is uniquely qualified to justify mankind because He is God (cf. Rom. 4:5). For this reason, we sing: "My hope is built on nothing less than Jesus' blood and righteousness." Otherwise, if Jesus is not God, we would be attributing our salvation not to God but to a creature.

Third, without the Trinity, our worship to God is idolatrous. Only God can be worshiped (cf. Ex. 20:3-5; Psa. 96:1-13; Rev. 4:11). Yet if Jesus is not God, and if the Holy Spirit is not God, our worship is sinful. Today we worship "by the Spirit" and "glory in Christ Jesus" (Phil. 3:3). We pray "in the name of Jesus" (John 14:13). Jesus is the recipient of worship both in the past (Matt. 2:11; 14:33; 21:1, 9; 28:9; Mark 16:1; John 12:13) and in the future (Phil. 2:9-11; Rev. 5:12-14). It is impossible to separate Jesus Christ and the Holy Spirit from our worship. If Jesus and the Spirit are not God, then they are just creatures and thus we are worshiping the creature rather than the Creator (Rom. 1:25).

Fourth, without the Trinity, we lose all satisfying reasons for our existence. What was God doing before Creation, and why did He create mankind? In the Trinity, we find the life-giving (cf. Jer. 2:13) Father loving the Son (John 17:24) and creating the world for Him (Col. 1:16) and for His glory (Eph. 1:6). If there is no Trinity, we see a God who is only one Person – a Person who creates so He can be a creator, who rules so He can be a ruler – a God who did not love before there was a creation to love.

Fifth, without the Trinity, we have no hope of religious unity. Christians are commanded to be united in the "same mind and the same judgment" (1 Cor. 1:10, cf. Phil. 2:2). Jesus prayed for this kind

---

23 Roy Lanier Sr., *The Timeless Trinity*, p. 59

of unity on the basis of the unity among the Godhead. He wished that Christians "may all be one, just as you, Father, are in Me, and I in you" (John 17:21). The reason there should be no religious denominations and sects within Christendom is because there are no such divisions within the Trinity. In fact, the model we use in the pursuit of unity of doctrinal beliefs should be the unity of beliefs held by the Father, Son, and Holy Spirit.

CONCLUSION

You might be thinking, "I'm still not sure I understand the Trinity very well." To which I say, "Welcome to the club!" Yet knowing God as a Trinity is the best way to understand what the Bible teaches about the Godhead. God is one in essence, and three in personality. Each eternal Person of the Godhead – Father, Son, and Holy Spirit, is fully God, and each Person has a role in the undivided single essence of God.

The thing that makes Christianity so distinct from other religions is the identity of our God.

There are sometimes similarities between Christianity and false religions that are invented by man. However, the thing that makes Christianity so distinct is the identity of our God. The foundation of our faith is built entirely upon God the Father, God the Son, and God the Holy Spirit. I could believe in doing good works; I could believe that a man named Jesus lived and was crucified two millennia ago; I could believe in salvation by grace alone through my obedient faith; I could believe all of the miracles recorded in the Bible. But if I do not believe in the one God as expressed in the three Persons of the Father, the Son, and the Holy Spirit, I cannot be a Christian.

DISCUSSION QUESTIONS

1. When the word **Godhead** appears in the English Bible, is it used specifically in reference to the triune nature of God?

2. Why is it not accurate to describe the Trinity with illustrations like a three-leaf clover, H_2O, or an egg?

3. Do we have to fully understand the triune personhood of God to accept it as true?

4. What was God doing before He created the world?

5. What single word best describes God?

6. What is **functional subordination**? How does it describe the Trinity? How does it describe the husband and wife marriage relationship?

7. Why is **modalism** false?

8. Why is **tritheism** false?

9. How is *modern feminism* an attack upon the Trinity?

10. How is *Calvinism* an attack upon the Trinity?

CHAPTER 5

WHO'S IN CHARGE HERE?

THE SOVEREIGNTY OF GOD

THE great king Nebuchadnezzar, while repenting for his failure to acknowledge God as the true reason for his prosperity, said,

> He does according to His will among the host of heaven and among the inhabitants of the earth; and none can stay His hand or say to Him, "What have you done? (Dan. 4:35)

Nebuchadnezzar, at the peak of his reign, had managed to build one of the largest and most powerful kingdoms the world had ever known. Yet God taught him that there was a heavenly kingdom so glorious and magnificent that it made Nebuchadnezzar's own kingdom look like a cheap foosball table.

The world's most powerful leaders – kings, presidents, prime ministers, dictators, czars, emperors, CEOs, generals – are mere rubber balls in God's pinball machine. And it doesn't stop with them; *everyone* and *everything* in the universe ultimately bows to God's good pleasure. No one can defeat God's plan (Isa. 14:27). This chapter is about God's governance over the world, known as His **sovereignty**.

WHAT IS GOD'S SOVEREIGNTY?

To put it briefly, *sovereign* means "having unlimited power or authority."[1] Yet God's sovereignty is more than His omnipotence – it is His *right* to it. *Sovereignty* is God's freedom to exercise His power and authority. Jack Cottrell writes,

---

1 Merriam-Webster.com

God's sovereignty may be concisely summed up as absolute lordship. It is equivalent to kingship or dominion: God has absolute dominion over all things; He is the God of gods, King of kings, and Lord of lords (Deut. 10:17; 1 Tim. 6:15-16; Rev. 19:16).[2]

"Sovereign" does not appear in the Bible, but the fact that God alone is sovereign permeates Scripture. God has unlimited power and authority over all things. The sovereignty of God is not a separate attribute of God, but a *result* of His attributes. *Because* God is omniscient, omnipotent, omnipresent, holy, just, loving, etc., God is thus sovereign over everything. That is, because God is God, He is thus Lord over all creation.

God came before all things (Col. 1:17; cf. Gen. 1:1); God created all things (John 1:3; Col. 1:16); God sustains all things (Heb. 1:3; Col. 1:17; Heb. 2:10); God transcends all things (Eph. 4:6; Psa. 8:1; 57:5); God knows all things (Psa. 147:5; Isa. 46:10; Rom. 11:33); God can do all things (Gen. 18:14; Jer. 32:27; Matt. 19:26); God owns all things (Psa. 24:1; Psa. 50:10; 1 Cor. 6:19). Therefore, God is sovereign and has a *right* to control all things.

God can do whatever He pleases (Psa. 135:6). All things ultimately work according to His Will (Eph. 1:11). God's plan always comes to pass (Isa. 46:9-10). The world's most powerful men are mere peons compared to God (Dan. 2:20-21; Job 12:18; Psa. 2:8-9; Prov. 21:1; Acts 12:23). No one can thwart God's purpose (Job 42:2; Dan. 4:35; Isa. 43:13).

Human language is easily exhausted as we try to fathom God's majestic, limitless greatness. Just try to picture the imagery Isaiah attempts to paint:

> Behold, the nations are like a drop from a bucket, and are accounted as the dust on the scales; behold, He takes up the coastlands like fine dust. [...] All the nations are as nothing before Him, they are accounted by Him as less than nothing and emptiness. [...] It is He who sits above the circle of the earth, and its inhabitants are like grasshoppers; who stretches out the heavens like a curtain, and

---

2 Jack Cottrell, *The Faith Once For All*, p. 80

spreads them like a tent to dwell in; who brings princes to nothing, and makes the rulers of the earth as emptiness. (Isa. 40:15, 17, 22-23)

We agree with Arthur Pink's description of God's sovereignty:

> The sovereignty of God—what do we mean by this expression? We mean the supremacy of God, the kingship of God, the God-hood of God. To say that God is sovereign is to declare that God is God. To say that God is sovereign is to declare that He is the Most High, doing according to His will in the army of heaven, and among the inhabitants of the earth, so that none can stay His hand or say unto Him what doest thou? (Dan. 4:35). To say that God is sovereign is to declare that He is the Almighty, the possessor of all power in heaven and earth, so that none can defeat His counsels.[3]

We believe in God's sovereignty, but at times we fail to appreciate it as we should. Perhaps some could be charged with talking about God's sovereignty only to offset the sectarian view of **divine determinism** (Calvinism).[4] And when we only think of divine sovereignty in terms of what it is *not* at the neglect of what it *is*, we end up with a very small view of God.

THE PARADOX OF GOD'S SOVEREIGNTY

A **paradox** is a statement that at first seems self-contradictory and impossible, but upon further investigation expresses a possible truth. If God's sovereignty is His right to "unlimited power or authority," why does it appear that there are things God does not have the power or authority to do? For example, if God is sovereign, why can He not make a boulder so large even He cannot move it? Why can He not make someone as old as Him? Why can He not create someone who is both unable to sin against Him and capable of free choice to love and serve Him? The reason is because these are all involve logical contradictions. It is not that God cannot do them, but rather that they *cannot be accomplished at all*. Genuine sovereignty operates within the bounds of rationality and logic. The fact that God wants us to reason

---

3 Arthur Pink, *The Sovereignty Of God*, p. 15(?)
4 See chapter 6

with Him (cf. Isa. 1:18) indicates that He Himself is rational.

We must further refine our understanding of God's sovereignty to mean unlimited power or authority "to do whatever is consistent with God's own perfection."[5] We did not pull this definition out of thin air; the Bible itself teaches this. For example, Isaiah 40:28 tells us that God *cannot* get tired. God Himself says that He *cannot* change (Mal. 3:6; Jas. 1:17). Paul tells us that God *cannot* deny Himself (2 Tim. 2:13). The Holy Spirit reminds us that God *cannot* lie (Heb. 6:18; Titus 1:2). James adds that God *cannot* be tempted with evil (Jas. 1:13). Norman Geisler writes,

> God can do whatever is *possible* to do – there are no limits on His power except that it be consistent with His own unlimited nature. He can do anything that does not involve a contradiction. The Bible describes Him as "the Almighty" in numerous places (e.g., Gen. 17:1; Exo. 6:3; Num. 24:4; Job 5:17). *He has all the might or power there is to have.* [6] (emp. added)

As we talk about God's sovereignty, two issues present a paradox: (1) the problem of sin,[7] and (2) the problem of pain and suffering.[8] At first glance, it seems absurd that a righteous God who is sovereign would allow sin and suffering to exist among His creation. Indeed, many have forfeited the faith because they did not understand the problem of sin and the problem of pain and suffering. But upon further examination, we can understand why the reality of sin and suffering in the world do not dethrone God of His sovereignty.

FINDING STRENGTH IN GOD'S SOVEREIGNTY

1. RESPECTING GOD'S SOVEREIGNTY DEEPENS OUR REVERENT FEAR OF GOD

Pay close attention: The last thing you want to do is offend a God who

---

5 Thomas B. Warren, *God and Evil*, p. 10
6 Norman Geisler, *Systematic Theology*, p. 679
7 Chapter 6
8 Chapter 7

is sovereign. To disappoint or sin against an infinite God is a horrific thought – far more terrifying than the most chilling horror film you could ever watch (Isa. 59:1-2; cf. Psa. 51:4). If we have wronged someone on earth, we can hide from that person and take precautions so that he or she cannot take revenge. But we cannot hide from God (Job 12:22), who will surely carry out divine justice (cf. Rom. 12:19; Heb. 10:30-31).

When we begin to understand God's sovereignty, we will either feel a deep sense of comfort knowing He is for us (Rom. 8:31), or we will be struck with gut-wrenching terror knowing He is against us (cf. Prov. 21:15). To be indifferent about God is to be ignorant of His sovereignty.

When we begin to understand God's sovereignty, we will either feel a deep sense of comfort knowing He is for us, or we will be struck with gut-wrenching terror knowing He is against us.

In Isaiah's vision of heaven, not even the creatures of heaven – untainted by human sin – could look upon God (Isaiah 6:1-8). If the angelic host are unable to look at God, how much more should lowly mankind bow before God in reverent awe? Psalm 89:5-7 says,

> Let the heavens praise your wonders, O Lord, your faithfulness in the assembly of the holy ones! For who in the skies can be compared to the Lord? Who among the heavenly beings is like the Lord, a God greatly to be feared in the council of the holy ones, and awesome above all who are around Him?

There is a silly (or blasphemous) idea among religious people today that God is a sort of "buddy" to them and speaks to them in the same nonchalant manner as another human being. I recall hearing a man tell me that God spoke to him one day when he was mowing his grass. To which I thought, "And you kept mowing your grass?" Whenever God manifests Himself to someone in the Bible, the person always stops whatever they are doing and begins to *tremble*.

Charles Spurgeon wrote,

> The holiest tremble in the presence of the thrice Holy One: their
> familiarity is seasoned with the profoundest awe. [...] Where angels
> veil their faces, men should surely bow in lowliest fashion. Sin is akin
> to presumptuous boldness, but holiness is sister to holy fear. [...]
> If mere creatures are struck with awe, the courtiers and favorites of
> heaven must be yet more reverent in the presence of the Great King.
> [...] Irreverence is rebellion. [...] and the more His glories are seen
> by us in that nearer access, the more humbly we prostrate ourselves
> before His majesty.[9]

2. RESPECTING GOD'S SOVEREIGNTY CHANGES HOW WE VIEW OUR FELLOW MAN

We will view every human being with greater dignity since man is
created in God's image:

> Then God said, "Let Us make man in Our image, after Our likeness.
> And let them have dominion over the fish of the sea and over the
> birds of the heavens and over the livestock and over all the earth and
> over every creeping thing that creeps on the earth." So God created
> man in His own image, in the image of God He created Him; male
> and female He created them. (Gen. 1:26-27)

Regardless of race, gender, or socio-economic status, every single
person bears the image of our sovereign God, thus the soul of man is
far more precious than all the wealth combined in this material world
(cf. Matt. 16:26).

3. RESPECTING GOD'S SOVEREIGNTY MOTIVATES US TO RESTORE NEW TESTAMENT CHRISTIANITY

He has given all men the sovereign choice of consciously submitting
to *His* sovereignty, and we do so when we become Christians and are
added to His kingdom (John 3:5). The very act of being spiritually
crucified with Christ (cf. Gal. 2:20) should be an acknowledgment of

---

9 Charles Spurgeon, *The Treasury Of David*, p. 26

God's sovereignty.

When we respect God's sovereignty, we are acknowledging His lordship over our lives. God the Son (cf. John 10:30) has been given "all authority" and therefore we are to "observe all that [He] has commanded" (Matt. 28:18-20; cf. John 5:19-20; 12:49-50). Therefore, it logically follows that the more we respect God's sovereignty, the more we will want to observe all of the commandments as recorded in Jesus Christ's last Will and Testament (Heb. 9:15-17).

> *The more we respect God's sovereignty, the more we will want to observe all of the commandments as recorded in Christ's last Will and Testament.*

A sovereign God is a God who knows best. After all, God created us (Gen. 1:26-27); everything He has given us is for our own good (cf. Deut. 6:24); He has given us His Word in the Bible (1 Cor. 2:4, 13), and it contains "all things that pertain to life and godliness" (2 Pet. 1:3) – everything we need.

Knowing this, mankind has two choices: (a) we can follow the teachings of God's Son and His apostles as closely as possible, or (b) we can rebel against God by modifying, minimizing, ignoring, adding to, or picking and choosing which teachings of God's Son and His apostles we will follow. In other words, we can follow the pattern of God's Word as closely as possible (cf. Acts 2:42; Rom. 6:17-18; 1 Cor. 4:6; 2 Thess. 2:3; 1 Tim. 4:1ff; 2 Tim. 1:13; 3:14; 4:1ff; Gal. 1:23; 2 John 9; Jude 3), or we can reject God's sovereignty by creating our own version of Christianity that fits our own animal preferences or innovative opinions (cf. Col. 2:23).

Commenting on this, Albert Barnes wrote:

> God knew best what things it was more conducive to piety for His people to observe; and we are most safe when we adhere most closely to what He has appointed, and observe no more days and ordinances than He has directed. There is much wickedness of heart at the bottom, and there is nothing that more tends to corrupt pure

religion.[10]

In His sovereignty, God has predestined that His Word be the standard by which we are judged (John 12:48). Why would any honest servant of God be so disloyal as to modify, diminish, or reform that Word?

4. RESPECTING GOD'S SOVEREIGNTY GIVES US COMFORT IN TIMES OF TROUBLE

As Christians, we have crucified our former selves (Gal. 5:24). Christ is now living in us (Gal. 2:20). Like Christ, we are now going about our Father's business (Luke 2:49). More than anything else, we want God's purpose to be accomplished (Matt. 6:10). And before He created the world, God's purpose was already planned and complete.

> For those whom He foreknew He also predestined to be conformed to the image of His Son, in order that He might be the firstborn among many brothers. And those whom He predestined He also called, and those whom He called He also justified, and those whom He justified He also glorified. (Rom. 8:29-30)

Nothing can ultimately keep God's Will from happening.

Knowing God is sovereign because of His divine communicable[11] and incommunicable[12] attributes – and desiring that God's Will be accomplished – the Christian can find deep comfort knowing that nothing can ultimately keep God's Will from happening. And those of us who are faithful to God (i.e. Christians) will be part of His plan and will thus be glorified.

Furthermore, knowing God is sovereign over the earth and its affairs, we are also given this promise:

> And we know that for those who love God all things work together for good, for those who are called according to His purpose. (Rom.

---

10 Albert Barnes, *Notes On The New Testament: Ephesians, Philippians, and Colossians*, p. 271
11 Chapter 2
12 Chapter 3

8:28)

Christians, and only Christians, can find peace in the knowledge that God – who will one day deliver us – notices our pain, suffering, and struggles.

5. RESPECTING GOD'S SOVEREIGNTY CAUSES US TO BELIEVE IN GOD'S PROVIDENCE

God did not create the world only to abandon it. No, God is very much active in His world. Jack Cottrell sums it up well:

> By "providence" we mean God's continuous activity of preserving and governing the universe by His knowledge, power, wisdom, and goodness, for the fulfillment of His purpose in creation. [...] Providence [...] deals with the ongoing history of the universe, and to God's continuing multiformed activity in it.[13]

God is actively protecting and guiding His creation (Matt. 6:26-30); God is actively sustaining His creation (Heb. 1:3; Col. 1:17); God is actively orchestrating the uniformity of His creation (cf. Gen. 8:22). Knowing God's providential work in the lives of His children (cf. Rom. 8:28), Christians can calmly face life's calamities.

> ...for He has said, "I will never leave you nor forsake you." So we can confidently say, "The Lord is my helper; I will not fear; what can man do to me?" (Heb. 13:5b-6)

Christians, and only Christians, can find peace in the knowledge that God — who will one day deliver us — notices our pain, suffering, and struggles.

---

13 Jack Cottrell, *The Faith Once For All*, p. 111

MISCONCEPTIONS ABOUT GOD'S SOVEREIGNTY

"WE SHOULD NOT STUDY THE BIBLE TO KNOW GOD'S SOVEREIGNTY."

There are many so-called believers in God today who do not think we should examine so closely the nature of God. Some even go so far as to claim that it is irrelevant – or even *irreverent* – to look at God so systematically. Notice the contempt one popular religious postmodern writer, Brian McLaren, has for our study:

> In the recent past we talked a lot about absolute truth, attempting to prove abstract propositions about God (for instance, proving the sovereignty of God). In the emerging culture, however, we will be much more interested in embodied truth (for instance, how Jesus demonstrated God's mercy), and we will want to convey real-life stories about God – stories from our lives as well as from the Bible.[14]

In other words, McLaren believes we shouldn't concern ourselves with studying to better understand the God of the Bible. No, instead we should study the so-called "God" of our experiences and feelings.

McLaren's words are so senseless and counter-intuitive that I struggle to understand them. It should go without saying that our understanding of God should define our experiences and feelings about Him, not the other way around. But above all, what McLaren said represents an incorrect view of Biblical faith.

In the Bible, having "faith" in God is never portrayed as believing in spite of logic or revelation. McLaren says you can have faith in God apart from Scripture. But that is not *faith*; that is *speculation*. His view (representative of an alarming number today) promotes irrationality and turns the study of God into intellectual mush. However, true faith in the Bible is based upon revealed evidence (cf. Acts 17:1-4; 11-12; Heb. 11:1-4; 2 Cor. 5:7).

---

14 Brian McLaren, *Adventures In Missing The Point*, p. 102

"GOD IS NOT SOVEREIGN BECAUSE EVIL AND SUFFERING EXIST IN THE WORLD."

The problem of sin and suffering is discussed in greater detail in chapters 6 and 7. However, we can briefly reply to this argument here. Simply because God has not yet crushed evil and stopped suffering does not mean He never will. Scripture affirms that God will eventually cause all sin and suffering to cease (cf. Rev. 21:4). In the meantime, in God's sovereignty, He has granted mankind the sovereign choice to serve Him. And as long as man has the ability to choose, it logically follows that there will be sin and suffering (because man often makes poor choices). God is patiently allowing time for whosoever will decide to repent (2 Pet. 3:9; Rev. 22:17).

"THE PRIMARY GOAL OF GOD AND HIS PEOPLE SHOULD BE TO FEED THE POOR, HEAL THE SICK, AND CORRECT THE SOCIAL INJUSTICES OF THE WORLD."

One may initially think, "What's wrong with this view? And what does it have to do with God's sovereignty?" Christians are commanded to help those who are destitute, hurting, and suffering. Jesus commanded us to look after our fellow man in His parable of the good Samaritan (cf. Luke 10:25-37). In keeping with this command, Christians have historically thrown themselves into the work of orphanages, inner-city community outreach, human rights advocacy, criminalizing the killing of unborn children, relieving third-world hunger and debt, and more. These forms of compassion should characterize God's people, since pure religion before God is "to visit orphans and widows in their affliction, and to keep oneself unstained from the world" (Jas. 1:27).

With all of that said, again we ask: "What is wrong with this view?" **This view confuses the problem with the symptom.** Instead of tackling the problem of sin, this view focuses on the consequences of the Fall – death, disease, poverty, and so on – and makes these things the big problems with which God and His people should primarily concern themselves. And if God's **primary** job is to ensure that the poor are fed and the sick are healed in this temporal world, He must surely not be sovereign because it would appear He is doing a very poor job. Yet a sovereign God never does a poor job at anything.

Surely, if God wanted to correct all the world's temporal problems, He could do so. With one word, Jesus could have healed the entire multitude of invalids at the Bethesda healing pool, but He didn't (cf. John 5:2-9). But God's primary goal is not to fix the world's social ills (not now, anyway). Those who obey His Son eagerly await salvation from all of this world's problems (Rom. 8:19-25). God's primary task, by means of His Son, is to save souls (Luke 19:10). Whoever freely chooses to believe and obey the Son will find this salvation (John 3:36).

> *If God's primary job is to ensure that the poor are fed and the sick are healed in this temporal world, He must surely not be sovereign because it would appear He is doing a very poor job.*

We must not reduce the mission of God and His people to the mere task of social justice and benevolence. Our sovereign God is primarily concerned about the eternal problem of sin and how it has severed mankind's relationship with Him (Isa. 59:1-2). We must not confuse the underlying problem (sin) with the consequences of the Fall (pain, suffering, death) and the ongoing effects of sin. We do not serve a God who is incapable of fixing this world's problems. In His sovereign time, all things will ultimately work together for good for those who have freely chosen to accept His offer of salvation (cf. Rom. 8:28).

CONCLUSION

God is a sovereign God, meaning He has the right to exercise His divine power and authority. If He were not sovereign, He would not be worthy of our worship. Instead, God's power and wisdom are beyond measure. Therefore, we take great comfort in being His children.

DISCUSSION QUESTIONS

1. What does **sovereignty** mean?

2. What makes God sovereign?

3. What is a **paradox**? And why is it a paradox that God is unable to do some things?

4. What is God unable to do?

5. If God is not sovereign, would He still be God? Why or why not?

6. What do you think the realization of God's sovereignty should do to us?

7. Can you have faith in God without acknowledging that He is sovereign?

8. How would you respond to someone who thinks it is counterproductive to study God's sovereignty?

9. What is one reason why evil and suffering exist in our world?

10. If the *primary* job of God and His people is to engage in social action, what does this say about God's sovereignty?

CHAPTER **6**

WHY DOES GOD ALLOW WICKEDNESS TO EXIST?

GOD'S SOVEREIGNTY & THE PROBLEM OF SIN

TWO of my peers from college – we will call them April and David – married soon after graduating. Their story quickly became a sad one. Over the following two years, April grew dissatisfied with her marriage and secretly began seeing another man. She eventually committed adultery and became pregnant with a child out of wedlock. When her sin became public knowledge, she repented and begged her husband not to divorce her. He graciously agreed, and together they made the deeply emotional, yet justifiable decision to give her baby up in an open adoption.

April has now become a vocal advocate of open adoptions for couples who have been devastated by pregnancies out of wedlock. However, recently, when recounting her story to some of her friends, she said, "God has very plainly put a path in front of me. Before now, I did not understand His plans for me, but I know now He intended for this to happen all along."

While April's motives are sincere, her understanding of God is gravely mistaken. Her words suggest that she believes God actually *predestined* her to commit fornication and thus she is not entirely responsible for her sin. If this is true, then it begs the question: Does God actually *cause* or *determine* people to sin?

SOVEREIGNTY ≠ DIVINE DETERMINISM

One very popular denominational preacher and writer, John Piper, is famous for saying that "all things" – even down to the subatomic level – "are ordained, guided, and governed" by God.[1] The idea that God determines *everything* can be traced back to Augustine of Hippo in the 5th century and is particularly popular among a branch of Protestantism known as **Reformed theology**.

Reformed theology, more commonly known as **Calvinism**[2] (we will use these words interchangeably), is a religious philosophy that follows the teachings of John Calvin and other Protestant theologians from the Reformation era. It is should be noted that Reformed theology, or Calvinism, is experiencing a resurgence in America today. So popular is Reformed theology that any Christian who reads relatively conservative denominational literature is well acquainted with famous Calvinistic authors. Understandably, younger preachers thirsty for truth tend to be particularly fond of their writings because of their often passionate, yet conservative, approach to many Biblical issues. (And as a result, their Calvinistic influences sometimes unknowingly creep into the young preacher's respective pulpit.)

The reason it is important to examine Calvinism as it relates to this study is because Reformed theology has traditionally emphasized God's sovereignty and predestination over everything else. In fact, the idea of the sovereignty of God is the basis of Calvinism itself. Reformed theologians take great pride in the lofty ways in which they talk about God. Ben Warburton writes, "The one rock upon which Calvinism builds is that of the absolute and unlimited sovereignty of the eternal and self-existent Jehovah."[3]

But herein lies the problem: The sovereign God of the Bible and the

---

1 John Piper, "Confronting The Problem Of Evil," DesiringGod.org
2 Calvinism, also known as *Reformed theology*, is basically the body of religious teachings and traditions started by John Calvin (1509 – 1564 A.D.) and other Reformation-era theologians such as Ulrich Zwingli and Jonathan Edwards. Calvinism can be summarized in five false religious ideas: (1) Total Depravity (babies are born guilty of the sin of their parents), Unconditional Election (God arbitrarily chooses – independent of any known standard - who will be eternally saved and who will be eternally damned), Limited Atonement (Christ did not die for everyone), Irresistible Grace (you do not have a choice as to whether or not you will obey the gospel), Perseverance of the Saints (it is impossible for a Christian to rebel against God).
3 Ben A. Warburton, *Calvinism*, p. 63

sovereign God of Calvinism are two very different Gods. Calvinists have redefined the meaning of the word *sovereignty*. To the Bible-believing Christian, *sovereignty* simply means God's ability and right to rule the world (chapter 5). However, to the devoted Calvinist, *sovereignty* means "divine determinism." **Divine determinism** is the belief that God determines, causes, and orchestrates *everything* in history according to His preconceived plan, *including sin and evil.*

Calvinists erroneously believe that God is the *reason* for sin, since – according to Calvinism – "sovereignty" is somehow synonymous with "total control." Thus, they create a false dichotomy,[4] claiming that if God is *sovereign*, He must orchestrate and control *everything that ever happens* – and if He does not control everything, He supposedly cannot be sovereign. Arthur Pink, a famous Calvinist, writes, "Only two alternatives are possible: God must either rule, or be ruled; sway, or be swayed; accomplish His own will, or be thwarted by His creatures."[5] In the words of Jack Cottrell, Calvinists "equate sovereignty with *causation*, and say that the only way for God to be sovereign is if He is the sole, ultimate cause or originator of everything that takes place, including events in the natural world as well as human decisions." Consequently, Cottrell continues, "there is no truly free will"[6] for mankind in the Calvinist worldview.

> *The sovereign God of the Bible and the sovereign God of Calvinism are two very different Gods.*

As a result, according to Calvinism, if someone commits a horrible atrocity, it is ultimately because God must have *willed* it to happen in the first place. Edwin Palmer, a well-known Calvinist, said it bluntly: God "has foreordained everything [...] – *even sin*."[7] How horrifying a thought. R.C. Sproul Jr., another leading Calvinist today, terrifyingly said, "God in some sense desired that man would fall into sin [...] *He*

---

4 A *dichotomy* (pronounced "die-kot-uh-mee") is the division of two mutually exclusive things or ideas. Thus, a *false dichotomy* is the division of two things or ideas that are not necessarily mutually exclusive. For example, it is a false dichotomy to say, "You either like bacon or sausage." Why? Because real men like both bacon and sausage.
5 Arthur Pink, *The Sovereignty Of God*, p. 14
6 Jack Cottrell, *The Faith Once For All*, p. 81
7 Edwin H. Palmer, *The Five Points Of Calvinism*, p. 25, emp. added.

created sin."[8] Chilling, right?

Just as egregious is the Calvinistic idea that God subjectively causes individuals to have faith. To the Calvinist, the words "I have personal faith in Christ Jesus" have no real meaning because God is supposedly the *cause* of all things. To the Calvinist, you cannot *choose* to have faith; God must put it in you. According to the *Synod of Dort*,[9] God chooses who will believe in Him and who will not.[10] This, of course, makes the words of Jesus powerless: "whoever believes in Him may have eternal life" (John 3:16). Why? Because you can't "believe in Him" without God *causing* you to believe in Him! To call this cruel would be an understatement. It is like dangling crutches at the top of the stairs, saying to a paraplegic below, "Come and get them!"

Historically, Christians have distinguished between God's sovereignty **de jure** and **de facto**. *De jure* is a Latin word which in this context refers to God's right to rule; *De facto* is a Latin word which in this context refers to God's meticulous control over all events. Ardent Calvinists see this distinction as a mere formality; they believe God is both sovereign *de jure* <u>and</u> *de facto* all the time. Yet, New Testament Christians have always acknowledged that God is always sovereign *de jure* and chooses to limit His sovereignty *de facto*. In other words, God has the ability to meticulously control everything, but in His wisdom and love for mankind, He has chosen *not* to determine everything *yet*.

We find the distinction between God's sovereignty *de jure* and *de facto* when Christ taught His disciples to pray, "Your will be done, on earth as it is in heaven" (Matt. 6:10). If God is already micro-managing every detail of history, why would anyone need to pray for God's will to be done on earth? If God is sovereign *de facto*, it would already be done.

Any honest observer must acknowledge that the Bible is permeated

---

8   R.C. Sproul Jr., *Almighty Over All*, p. 53

9   The *Synod of Dort* was a very important meeting in denominational history ultimately deciding the future of Calvinism. It was held between the years 1618-1619 in the town of Dordrecht ("Dort") in the Netherlands. The Synod of Dort was held to silence honest, Scriptural challenges to Calvinism, and at its conclusion the traditional five points of Calvinism were formalized, namely: Total Depravity, Unconditional Election, Limited Atonement, Irresistible Grace, and the Perseverance of the Saints.

10 See Article XIV of *The Articles Of The Canons of Dort* (1619). "Faith is the gift of God; not in that it is offered to the will of man by God, but that the thing itself is conferred on him, inspired, infused into him. Not even that God only confers the power of believing, but from thence expects the consent, or the act of believing: but that He, who worketh both to will and to do, worketh in man both to will to believe, and to believe itself, [...] and thus He worketh all things in all." (Translated By Thomas Scott, p. 301).

with the implication that God has given men the choice to serve Him. We could fill this book with examples of God giving mankind the freedom of choice. How otherwise could God extend His kindness if people are unable to choose repentance (Rom. 2:4)? How otherwise can we be commanded to "grow in the grace" of the Lord Jesus Christ if are unable to choose to do so (2 Pet. 3:18)? Why would Joshua tell the Israelites to choose whom they would serve if they could not actually choose (Josh. 24:15)? How could God not "show partiality" if He individually chooses on whom to force faith (Acts 10:34)? How calloused is God if He "commands all men everywhere to repent" if they are unable to repent (Acts 17:30)?

Let's be very clear: You can be entirely dedicated to the doctrine of God's sovereignty while simultaneously being absolutely sure of mankind's free choice.

The Bible does, in fact, teach that God is sovereign, but it certainly does not teach that God determines mankind's decisions and preordains mankind's actions. Let's be very clear: You can be entirely dedicated to the doctrine of God's sovereignty while simultaneously being absolutely sure of mankind's free choice.

But we have not fully answered the question: Why does God's sovereignty allow sin to exist?

WHY DOES SIN EXIST?

The first paradox of God's sovereignty is the problem of sin. The stinging question is this: If God is truly sovereign over the affairs of the earth, why does He allow evil to exist? If God has all power and authority, does this make God responsible for sin?

At first glance, this seems like a serious problem. If God is truly sovereign, then He has all power and authority. And if God has all power and authority, why does He allow mankind to sin?

What Calvinists have failed to affirm is the Bible's answer to this important question: God can grant mankind personal freedom without losing His sovereignty. Or, to say it another way, as God rules His creation, He has granted mankind the liberty to serve Him or rebel against Him. This fact has been evident since the beginning of time.

IN THE BEGINNING: MADE IN HIS IMAGE

As we open the book of Genesis, we find God stepping onto the stage, setting the universe in motion. "And God said, 'Let there be light,' and there was light" (Gen. 1:3). Then on day 2 – He made the skies; Day 3 – He made land and vegetation; Day 4 – He made the galaxies; Day 5 – He made fish and birds. And so on and so forth. Soon we find a new creature being introduced: man. On day 6, God picked up a small pile of dirt, formed it and breathed life into it, and human life was created. You and I are ultimately just dust that has been brought to life by the breath of God (Gen. 3:19; Ecc. 3:20). Genesis 1:26-28 tells us the terms on which human beings were made:

> Then God said, "Let Us make man in Our image, after Our likeness. And *let them have dominion* over the fish of the sea and over the birds of the heavens and over the livestock and over all the earth and over every creeping thing that creeps on the earth." *So God created man in His own image, in the image of God He created him;* male and female He created them. And God blessed them. And God said to them, "Be fruitful and multiply and fill the earth and *subdue* it, and have *dominion* over the fish of the sea and over the birds of the heavens and over every living thing that moves on the earth. (emp. added)

Here we find one of the deepest truths in the Bible: We have been created in the image of God to rule over God's creation. Austin Fischer writes, "The implication is plain: within certain limitations, God empowers us to rule as He rules and this is what it means to have been created in His image."[11] Robert Morey wrote that this means "man was created to be and do on a finite level what God was and did on an

---

11 Austin Fischer, *Young, Restless, No Longer Reformed*, p. 64

infinite level."[12] Humanity has been entrusted with the responsibility of ruling over creation as God Himself would rule over it. In the words of Psalm 115:16, "The heavens are the Lord's heavens, but the earth He has given to the children of man."

Our sovereign God is so magnificently *giving* that He wanted to share a slice of His sovereignty with man. "What is man, that thou art mindful of him?" (Psa. 8:4).

THEN MAN SINNED

Then came the tree episode, which we all knew was bound to happen. God gave Adam and his wife an entire forest of trees, yet two were set apart: the tree of life and the tree of knowledge of good and evil (Gen. 2:9). He could eat from any tree – *except* the tree of knowledge of good and evil (Gen. 2:16-17). God told them not to eat from that tree; yet ultimately, they could choose to disobey Him. Adam did just that, and the rest is history.

Notice that Adam existed by the pure grace of God and was given free reign over the earth, but that freedom had some terms and conditions listed in the small print. Adam and his wife were free to obey or disobey God, but if they chose to disobey, the penalty would be death.

When Adam and his wife ate of the tree of knowledge of good and evil, did God somehow lose His sovereignty? In no way! When they disobeyed Him, God exercised His sovereignty by executing appropriate punishments that still exist today. God's sovereignty is in no way jeopardized by His allowing mankind a degree of freedom. Likewise, a parent's sovereignty over his child is in no way threatened when the child disobeys and the parent performs appropriate punishment.

Was God surprised by their actions? No! God knew man would sin,

12 Robert Morey, *Death and the Afterlife*. p. 37

and already had a plan for man's redemption before He brought man into existence (Acts 2:23; Eph. 1:4; 1 Pet. 1:20; cf. Gen. 3:15). Thomas B. Warren writes,

> ...It was not evil for God to create man with the freedom (of will) which enables him to do evil. To have created him without such freedom would have made of man nothing higher than a robot or a puppet. In such a case, man would not have been a moral being. But, once God had created man with freedom of will, He could not prevent (in the strict sense) his sinning without destroying man as man. It was not evil for God to create man with the power to do evil (sin) and to inflict pain and suffering, for such power is necessary for the power to do good. And, it is better that man should be than that he should not be.[13]

Today, God has granted us the ability to choose whether we will obey Him or reject Him (cf. Josh. 24:15). We can choose to be saved by His Son, or we can choose to be eternally separated from Him (2 Thess. 1:8). F. LaGard Smith writes, "When it is God Himself laying down the terms and conditions whereby His grace will be dispensed, His sovereignty is not even remotely threatened."[14]

AN ODD KIND OF SOVEREIGNTY

We serve a God who is quite unlike any god man could have dreamed up. He is sovereign over all creation, but He has demonstrated His sovereignty – not by absolute control, but by sharing His power with His creation for the sake of a relationship with Him. Fischer writes,

> God is always sovereign, but that means He – and not we – gets to decide what shape that sovereignty takes. And apparently, God's sovereignty makes room for human freedom so that God and humans can have a personal, and not merely casual, relationship.[15]

God's sovereignty does not mean that God desires to micro-manage every decision or action we take. He *could*; thus reducing us to mere

---

13 Thomas B. Warren, *God and Evil*, p. 306
14 F. LaGard Smith, *Troubling Questions for Calvinists*, p. 58
15 Austin Fischer, *Young Restless, No Longer Reformed*, p. 67

automatons or robots. But God has chosen to empower us as free-moral agents. God's sovereignty means He has sovereignty to do whatever He *wants* to do. And "whatever the Lord pleases, He does" (Psa. 135:6), including creating mankind with the ability to *choose* to love Him.

Perhaps nothing better illustrates the sovereignty of God than His own Son. Paul writes:

> Have this mind among yourselves, which is yours in Christ Jesus, who, though He was in the form of God, did not count equality with God a thing to be grasped, but emptied Himself, by taking the form of a servant, being born in the likeness of men. And being found in human form, He humbled Himself by becoming obedient to the point of death, even death on a cross. (Phil. 2:5-8)

God's sovereignty does not mean that God desires to micro-manage every decision or action we take.

God the Son, the Creator of the Universe (cf. John 1:3), chose to empty Himself. Jesus, having all the sovereign power and authority of God Himself, chose to give these things away.

Here we find a picture of God Himself. Jesus demonstrated what God has been like since the beginning of time. God limited His sovereignty with mankind when He created them in Genesis 1, and God limited His sovereignty as He lay in that manger (Luke 2:7). God shared His sovereignty with mankind when He gave mankind the tree of knowledge of good and evil, and God shared His sovereignty with mankind as He hung on that tree at Calvary (Acts 5:30).

Roger Olson sums it up best:

> Doesn't this limit God's power and sovereignty? No, because God remains omnipotent; He *could* control everything and everyone if He chose to. For the sake of having real, personal creatures who can freely choose to love Him or not, God limits His control. Still, God is sovereign in the sense that nothing at all can ever happen that God does not allow. Nothing falls totally outside of God's supervening

oversight and governance.[16]

THE REASON FOR SIN

When God chose to give mankind the ability to choose, inherent was the possibility that man would choose to reject God. But this ability to choose is necessary if we are to serve God with a sincere heart. The only way for evil **not** to exist would be for God to strip man of his ability to choose to do right or wrong. And evidently, most people ultimately want to do wrong (John 3:20; cf. Matt. 7:13-14).

God wants all men to be saved, and therefore He must consider Himself victorious when even just one person chooses to serve Him over Satan.

Not even God in His sovereignty could create creatures who were both free moral agents and who are guaranteed to obey Him. It is logically *impossible.* "Free moral agency" and "guarantee" are exclusive of one another.

God is a realist. In His foreknowledge, He knows that the majority of people will be lost (Matt. 7:13-14). But not only is He a realist, He is also an optimist. God is love (1 John 4:8), and love "believes all things, hopes all things" (1 Cor. 13:7). God wants all men to be saved (2 Pet. 3:9), and therefore He must consider Himself victorious when even just one person chooses to serve Him over Satan.

ANSWERING FALSE IDEAS ABOUT GOD'S SOVEREIGNTY

"I LOVE HOW REFORMED THEOLOGIANS TALK SO MUCH ABOUT GOD'S SOVEREIGNTY."

I occasionally hear fellow preachers comment on their love for how

---

16 Roger Olson, *Against Calvinism*, p. 100

preachers and writers in Reformed denominational churches talk so extravagantly and reverently about God. I, too, share their sentiment. It is refreshing to hear people in our dark world pay any kind of respect to our Creator. Certainly, all Christians can make room for more grandiose thoughts about God.

However, what is ironic is the fact that Calvinists revere the sovereignty of God while simultaneously undermining it. F. LaGard Smith writes:

> For all its admirable emphasis on the sovereignty of God, the irony is that Reformed theology ends up renouncing that very sovereignty when it refuses to acknowledge that such a sovereign God has it within His sovereign power to create beings who have both the personal freedom and responsibility to choose between good and evil.[17]

The person who holds only to the Bible has a much higher understanding of God's glorious sovereignty than the person who is encumbered by the snares of Calvinism. The God of Calvinism is truly a small god, for he is incapable of foreknowing the future without also foreordaining the future. However, the God of the Bible knows the future, but at the same time affords you the ability to make personal decisions. That, in a word, is love.

"THE STORY OF THE BIBLE IS ALL ABOUT GOD'S SOVEREIGNTY."

Everything we do should ultimately be about God's glory. "To Him be glory in the church and in Christ Jesus throughout all generations, forever and ever" (Eph. 3:21). Yet, if preaching the "sovereignty of God" causes us to minimize man's responsibility in choosing righteousness, we have allowed one truth in the Bible to cannibalize another. The wise student of the Bible does not let one Biblical teaching destroy another. G.K. Chesterton said it well,

> The heretic (who is also a fanatic) is not a man who loves truth too much; no man can love truth too much. The heretic is a man who

---

17 F. LaGard Smith, *Troubling Questions for Calvinists*, p. 22

loves his truth more than truth itself. He prefers the half-truth that he has found to the whole truth which humanity has found.[18]

The prevalence of Calvinism in religious literature today should always remind us of the ever-present danger of imbalance in our own theology. And the belief of Calvinism among men who are otherwise highly intelligent (certainly more so than me) should humble us enough to constantly scrutinize our own deeply held convictions in light of the Bible.

"ROMANS CHAPTER 9 TEACHES THAT GOD PREDESTINES PEOPLE."

Perhaps the Calvinist's favorite passage is Romans 9. If you segregate chapter 9 from the rest of Romans and do not know the historical context of Paul's words, it does in fact appear to corroborate their beliefs. But a close examination of the passage teaches the very *opposite* of what Calvinists have perverted it to mean.

In Romans 9, Paul begins by grieving over the fact that the majority of the Hebrew people are lost, despite all of the blessings God has given them (Rom. 9:1-5). God had chosen to give the Israelites the "oracles of God" (Rom. 3:2) and to bring Christ into the world through the bloodline of Abraham, Isaac, and Jacob (Rom. 9:5). Yes, God made Israel into a great nation (Rom. 9:6-9), but certainly not because of Israel's own merit; He was just fulfilling His promise to Abraham (Deut. 7:7-8).

Were there other men besides Abraham whom God could have blessed? Yes. Could God just as easily have chosen Esau over Jacob? Yes. But just as a teacher might randomly select a student on the first day of class to run an errand down the hall to benefit the entire class, God chose *someone* through whom the whole world could be blessed according to His divine plan. God chose Jacob, not for salvation, but for a special purpose (Rom. 9:10-13). The Jews, Paul's subject in Romans 9, felt that God chose them on the basis of merit – an

---

18 G. K. Chesterton, *The Common Man*, p. 22

arrogant attitude like the Pharisee in Luke 18:9-14. When Paul says that God "hated" Esau and "loved" Jacob (Rom. 9:13), He is merely using an oriental figure of speech, much like Jesus used in Luke 14:26, indicating greater versus lesser.

This is the point that Calvinists lose: Jacob was not saved because he received the honor of Christ's bloodline, nor was Esau lost by it. God did not choose to save one brother while condemning the other, just as God did not save all the Jews while condemning all the Gentiles. The Jews were wrong in thinking that God's choice of Jacob as a *physical nation* had anything to do with their *spiritual salvation* (Rom. 2:1-3).

Paul, in Romans 9, is not discussing personal, individual salvation. Rather, He is discussing God's election of a certain nation for a certain work. And in anticipation of the Jews being upset about this, Paul reminds them that God alone is sovereign (Rom. 9:14-18) and He alone has the right to set the conditions for salvation (cf. Rom. 1:17; 2:12-13).

> *Paul, in Romans 9, is not discussing personal, individual salvation. Rather, He is discussing God's election of a certain nation for a certain work.*

CONCLUSION

God, in His sovereignty, has chosen to share some of His sovereignty with those whom He made in His image. For man to have the freedom to love and serve God, man must logically also have the freedom to disobey and sin against God. Because God loves us and wants to sincerely be loved in return, God in His grace has given man this choice.

What is truly remarkable is not just that God has given mankind the ability to choose righteousness or evil, but that God can use even the most evil decisions for good (Rom. 8:28). Not even the most rebellious of people can ultimately thwart God's eternal purposes. It is simply

our decision to make – a luxury afforded to us only by God's grace –
whether we want to reap the rewards of God's offer of salvation.

In the words of the traditional blues song, sang throughout the years
by artists like Led Zeppelin, Nina Simone, Willie Nelson, and Van
Morrison,

> If I die and my soul be lost
> It's nobody's fault but mine
> Nobody's fault but mine
> Nobody's fault but mine

DISCUSSION QUESTIONS

1. Where did the idea that God determines everything originate?

2. What is **divine determinism?**

3. Why would it be tempting to believe that God determines everything, even down to the smallest atom?

4. What critical mistake do Calvinists make in defining **sovereignty?**

5. What is the difference between God's sovereignty **de jure** and **de facto?**

6. What does it mean that man is made in the image of God (Gen. 1:26-27)?

7. Why do you think God gave mankind the ability to choose?

8. What Biblical example do you think best illustrates God, in His sovereignty, choosing to limit His power?

9. Do you think it diminishes God's power in any way to share some of His sovereignty with man? Why or why not?

10. Does Romans 9 prove *divine determinism?* Why or why not?

CHAPTER 7

WHY DOES GOD ALLOW SUFFERING TO EXIST?

GOD'S SOVEREIGNTY & THE PROBLEM OF PAIN

WHEN the fire burns down your house – when the doctor diagnoses you with an aggressive form of cancer – when your spouse is killed in a car accident – when the nurse comes back with the blood-test results and informs you that your unborn baby likely has Down's syndrome – will your view of God sustain you in that time?

Why do such bad things happen in a world created by such a good God? When your world comes crashing down, you will not be interested in therapeutic theories and false ideas that can only bring temporary hope. More than anything else, you will want the closure and security that only knowledge of the "God of all comfort" (2 Cor. 1:3) can provide. When you lose everything that matters to you, will you "curse God and die" (Job 2:9), or will you respond like Job?

> Then Job arose and tore his robe and shaved his head and fell on the ground and worshiped. And he said, "Naked I came from my mother's womb, and naked shall I return. The Lord gave, and the Lord has taken away; blessed be the name of the Lord." In all this Job did not sin or charge God with wrong. (Job 1:20-22)

As we grow in our understanding of God's attributes – such as His omniscience, omnipresence, and omnipotence – it is equally important that we understand how God governs His creation. Otherwise, we risk an imbalanced view of God that could lead to unbelief when tragedy strikes. This chapter is about God's sovereignty over the world;

specifically how we can reconcile His sovereignty with the reality of pain and suffering.

THE PROBLEM OF PAIN
(OR, WHY DOES IT NOT ALWAYS SEEM LIKE OUR LOVING GOD IS IN CONTROL?)

The problem discussed in this chapter is not an easy one. It goes something like this:

1. If God is sovereign, He has the power to end all pain and suffering in the world.

2. If God is all-loving, He would *want* to end all pain and suffering in the world.

3. The reality is there is still a tremendous amount of pain and suffering in the world.

4. Therefore, God is either (a) not sovereign, (b) not all-loving, or (c) neither sovereign nor all-loving.

Put in simple terms, this is the problem of pain. Or, at least what *seems* like a problem. We shall see, however, that this logic is faulty.

When you face the bitter pains of life, how do you answer them? How do you reconcile, "I know the God of the Bible is real and loves me," with, "I know that I suffer"? The reality of pain and suffering in the world is another paradox as we seek to better understand our all-loving, sovereign God.

THE DIFFERENCE BETWEEN EVIL AND SUFFERING

Pain and suffering are sometimes the result of moral evil, though not always. Sometimes pain and suffering result from physical calamity, which is not *morally* evil. Mosquitos, earthquakes, tornados, and forest fires are morally neutral in and of themselves, though they often cause various degrees of suffering. One may look at the devastating effects of a flood and feel that the flood is evil, but that would be a misappropriation of the word "evil."

We must always remember that the only real evil is sin. In the words of Thomas B. Warren, who has written a great deal on the subject of pain and suffering:

> Sin (disobedience to God's Will as revealed in the Scriptures, that which contradicts sonship and brotherhood, that which involves the loss of fellowship with God) is the only real evil, that nothing subhuman is really evil, that man is responsible for his own sins, that evil (sin) really does exist, and that while it is the case that evil really does exist it is not evil that there is evil.[1]

Suffering, though sometimes the result of evil, is not evil in and of itself. The doctor who must amputate an arm, for example, is not responsible for evil; he is responsible for good (saving a life). Feeling pain after accidentally placing your hand on the eye of a hot stove is not evil; the pain felt was a good thing – otherwise you would not have been alerted to the fact that your hand was being burnt.

We now understand that suffering is not inherently evil. Yet, by definition, suffering hurts. So then why does God allow it?

WRONG ANSWERS TO THE PROBLEM OF PAIN

"THE GOD OF THE BIBLE DOES NOT EXIST."

Yet, if there is no God, nothing can be truly "right" or "wrong." But when we read about the thousands of bodies floating in the water after the Indonesian tsunami of 2004 – when we see footage of people jumping to their deaths from the fiery heights of the World Trade Center buildings during the 2001 terrorist attacks – when we see images of parents screaming in the parking lot during the Sandy Hook

---

1   Thomas B. Warren, *God and Evil*, p. 301

Elementary School massacre in 2012 – even the atheist cannot help but think, "This is not right."

The very utterance of those words betrays the fact that there is a God. When we say, "This is not right," we are not expressing a mere opinion or preference. We are in fact making a judgment about reality. Evil, pain, and suffering are all departures from how things *ought* to be. It logically follows that if there is a way things *ought* to be, then there must also be a *design* or *plan* for the world. And if there is a *design* or *plan* for the world, there must be a *Designer* or *Planner* behind it all.

Some may think that the reality of pain and suffering in the world implies that God must not exist. But what does it mean to assert that there is no God when our conviction that things are not right is so overwhelming? The problem of pain and suffering does not disprove the existence of God — the problem of pain and suffering actually *proves* that God exists. The evidence for the existence of God is overwhelming (cf. Rom. 1:19-20). Only a fool could deny it (Psa. 14:1; 53:1).

"GOD IS NOT IN CONTROL."

Some suggest that pain and suffering exist because God is not in control. However, this cannot be a true answer if we are also to believe the Bible. The Bible clearly affirms that God is in control of the world. For example, God rules the nations of men and disposes of them according to His divine standard (cf. Psa. 22:28; Prov. 14:34; Jer. 18:7-10; Dan. 2:21; 4:17). The abundance of miracles recorded in both the Old and New Testaments reveals that God is so in control of the world that He can suspend the natural laws of nature at His pleasure (e.g. Josh. 10:12-13; Matt. 21:14; Acts 3:7-11; etc.). God's control of universe upholds the very fabric of the cosmos (Heb. 1:3). Because God is in control, He can do anything He wills (Eph. 3:20). The story of Job illustrates that not even Satan can operate beyond the limits imposed upon him by God (cf. Heb. 2:14-15). Nothing that has happened or will happen in the world can ever thwart God's purpose.

You cannot believe the notion that God is not in control while simultaneously believing in the witness of the Bible.

"GOD IS NOT LOVING."

This answer to the problem of pain suggests God is apathetic to the world's problems. This cannot be true, however, since the Bible testifies to the fact that "God is love" (1 John 4:8). Nothing better illustrates the extent of God's concern for mankind than Him sending His Son into the world to redeem us from sin (John 3:16; Rom. 5:7-8; Eph. 2:1-5). John declares, "By this we know love, that He laid down His life for us" (1 John 3:16).

While standing at the foot of the cross, watching Jesus in unimaginable agony on those blood-soaked beams of wood, a scene which we are unworthy to even approach, are we so fickle to question God's love for us when – in our simple, limited minds – we do not always fully understand why we are suffering? Just because we may not understand the reason does not mean there *isn't* a reason (cf. Psa. 139:6; 145:3; Isa. 55:8-9; Rom. 11:33-36). The testimony of Calvary gives closure to our doubts about God's love. And because God so obviously cares for you personally, you can cast "all your anxieties on Him" (1 Pet. 5:7).

"GOD IS EVIL."

In other words, this explanation suggests that God is a malevolent deity, perhaps even taking pleasure in our pain. However, John reminds us, "in Him is no darkness at all" (1 John 1:5). The psalmist rhetorically asks, speaking of the Lord, "of whom shall I be afraid?" (Psa. 27:1). "No good thing does He withhold" (Psa. 84:11b). Peter exclaims, "Taste and see that the Lord is good!" (1 Pet. 2:3).

Jesus affirmed God's goodness when speaking to the rich young ruler (Matt. 19:17; Mark 10:18; Luke 18:19). God's goodness is praised throughout the Psalms (25:8; 34:8; 86:5; 100:5; 118:1; 136:1;

145:9) and is one of the bedrock truths of all of Scripture. You cannot believe God is evil while also believing in the Bible.

"ALL SUFFERING IS PUNISHMENT FOR PERSONAL SINS."

Without a doubt, *some* suffering – perhaps more than we want to admit – is a consequence of personal sin. For example, the married woman who has been infected with a sexually transmitted because she had an affair is suffering as a result of her personal sins. The immoral nation with a corrupt welfare system, handing out free money to lazy, gluttonous deadbeats, will eventually reap devastating economic consequences if it does not repent. The man who is fired for stealing from his company deserved the discipline he received.

Yet not all disease, sickness, hardship, and death is a result of personal sin. Whose fault is it when a man – who has eaten healthy and exercised his entire life – is diagnosed with cancer? Jesus reminded His disciples of this when they incorrectly believed that a man was born blind because of his sin or his parents' sin (John 9:1-3). The book of Job should remind us to guard against the idea that all suffering is punishment from God for one's personal sins (cf. Job 4:7-9). Instead, we must always humble ourselves before God and trust Him to see us through life's darkest hours, since we cannot always understand why things happen to us in this life.

> *One of the worst things you can say to someone grieving the loss of property, health, or a loved one is, "All things happen for a reason."*

"ALL THINGS HAPPEN FOR A REASON."

If beneath this statement lies the implication that *God* is the reason something happened, then this statement is wrong. In fact, one of the worst things you can say to someone grieving the loss of property, health, or a loved one is, "All things happen for a reason." Sometimes things just happen because they happen – not because God has a specific design behind a particularly unfortunate event. There does not need to be an immediate divine cause behind *everything*.

For example, God was not the cause, nor was He pleased, when Islamist Syed Farook and his wife murdered 16 social workers at the Inland Regional Center in San Bernardino, California on December 2, 2015. Of course, that terrible event in no way thwarted God's purpose (cf. Psa. 2:1-4), and perhaps there are mysterious ways God could have used that event for good (cf. Rom. 8:28). But God did not orchestrate that tragedy. God does not cause such wicked events.

But why did God not stop that mass shooting (or *any* mass shooting)? For the same reason God does not stop you from fudging the amount you owe on your taxes this year, texting on your phone while driving, or living a godless lifestyle; the same reason He does not stop you from cheating on your spouse or ignoring the needs of your neighbor. The freedom to make choices (often catastrophic choices) is an essential part of what it means to be human. Thomas B. Warren writes,

> Once man has been created, it is not the case that God could either *permit* or *prevent* man's sinning without so changing man's nature that he would no longer be man.[2]

Calvinists get this subject wrong by claiming that God *directly* causes *all things* to happen. On September 17th, 2001, six days after Islamic terrorists flew jetliners into the World Trade Center towers, the Pentagon, and a field in Pennsylvania, John Piper boldly said that God "could" and "would" be behind these actions.[3] According to Piper, and all other staunch Calvinists, all things happen for a reason, and *God* is that reason. Piper reiterates, "That is what the Bible teaches. God 'works all things after the counsel of His will' (Eph. 1:11)."[4] What a chilling thought – that *God* is ultimately behind all tragedies!

This is a disastrous abuse of the context of the apostle Paul's words

---

2 Thomas B. Warren, *God and Evil*, p. 298
3 John Piper, "Why I Do Not Say, 'God Did Not Cause the Calamity, but He Can Use It for Good'"
4 Ibid.

in Ephesians 1:11. We should note that Paul did not say, "God directs all things, period" – but rather that God has entirely ("all things") fulfilled His plan to redeem mankind and establish His church through Jesus His Son. This fact that Jesus redeemed us and established His church is the context of Ephesians 1 – not the divine orchestration of every individual event, wicked events included.

Along the same vein of thought, when a parent or sibling is grieving the loss of a child, sometimes a well-meaning friend will say something to the effect of, "God needed another angel in heaven." This horrifying statement not only reflects deep biblical ignorance (human beings do not go on to become angels, cf. Heb. 2:7), but it also leaves the terrifying impression that God is the direct cause of the child's death. Thank God He doesn't "need more angels."

There are Biblical explanations as to why there is suffering (including the loss of property, health, and innocent life) in this world. We will be discussing those reasons in the next few paragraphs. We should understand that God has given mankind freedom of choice, and sometimes bad choices are accompanied by tragic consequences – at times involving innocent people. Bear in mind, however, that God has a plan for people that is bigger than this temporal world. But the notion that God directly, individually ordains each and every instance of this world's pain and suffering is not Biblical.

THEN WHY IS THERE SO MUCH PAIN AND SUFFERING IN THE WORLD?

FIRST, SUFFERING IS AN INEVITABLE BYPRODUCT OF GOD'S STORY OF REDEMPTION FOR THE WORLD.

God did not create mankind with the naïve expectation that every man and woman would love Him in return. Of course, God *could have* forced everyone to love Him and submit to Him in perfect obedience. But had He done that, it would not have been love; it would have been robotics. The greatest thing we can ever do is love and serve God, and we do so by obeying Him from the heart (cf. Mark 12:30; Ecc. 12:13; John 14:15; 1 John 5:3). This necessitates that mankind be given the freedom of choice. God could not have created rational beings in His own image without also giving them genuine freedom.

It logically follows that if mankind has the freedom to *choose to love God*, mankind must also have the freedom to *choose to disobey God*. Mankind can choose to abuse the power he has been given (cf. Gen. 2:28-31). Today, mankind has proven to be most adept at wickedness. And disobedience to God naturally brings suffering – not only to the perpetrators, but even to the innocent.

Again, God was not surprised when mankind first sinned against Him in the garden (Gen. 2:15-17; 3:1-7). In fact, God in His omniscience knew it would happen all along – long before He created man. So before man ever sinned – before God even created the world – God planned a story of redemption from the sin and suffering that would naturally result from mankind's freedom of choice (Eph. 1:4; 3:11; 1 Pet. 1:20). God gave us grace in Christ Jesus "before the ages began" (2 Tim. 1:9). God did not will for there to be sin, but He did will for His grace to deliver us from that sin.

> *God did not will for there to be sin, but He did will for His grace to deliver us from that sin.*

Not only is suffering in this temporal world an inevitable byproduct of mankind's freedom of choice, but it also serves as an effective reminder of our need for redemption (Rom. 8:22-25). Suffering is a wake-up call to the fact that our present world is not all there is, and we eagerly await deliverance. Dr. Dave Miller writes,

> Human existence on earth was not intended to be permanent. [...] Suffering due to natural disasters and the like provide people with conclusive evidence that life on earth is brief and uncertain. They help us to distinguish the temporary from the permanent. In the face of physical calamities, and the host of other features of the created order that can cause suffering, we humans would do well to contemplate our

own fragility and finitude, and be driven to look beyond ourselves, and beyond the here and now, to a Higher Power who can inform us as to the meaning and purpose of life. Life is precarious – tomorrow may be too late.[5]

Suffering is a necessary consequence in a world of creatures blessed with free, moral choice. Yet without suffering, we would have no pressing reason to look to the hereafter.

SECOND, GOD SUBJECTED CREATION TO FUTILITY.

Does it not strike you as odd that when Adam and Eve sinned against God, God struck the earth with a curse, too? Those who think God over-reacted do not understand what it means to sin against a holy, infinite God. When Adam sinned, Adam told God, in essence, "I don't trust you anymore to provide for my life, and therefore I am going to rebel against your love and wisdom. For now on, I am going to do things my way." That was an insult to the glory of God, and it merited millennia full of pain and suffering. Just that one act of rebellion towards an infinite God was worthy of all the world's misery we experience still to this day (even if we personally are not guilty of that sin).

When Adam and Eve sinned morally, God punished the natural world physically.

It is worthy of note that even human beings punish moral wrongs with physical punishment. Parents often discipline their children physically when their children misbehave morally (cf. Prov. 13:24; 22:15; 23:13-14; 24; cf. Eph. 6:4; Heb. 12:5-11). Governments often inflict physical forms of discipline on citizens for their moral crimes (cf. Rom. 13:1-7; cf. 1 Pet. 4:15-16). Likewise, when Adam and Eve sinned morally, God punished the natural world physically. Paul writes,

> For I consider that the sufferings of this present time are not worth comparing with the glory that is to be revealed to us. For the creation

---

5 Dave Miller, *Why People Suffer*, p. 21

waits with eager longing for the revealing of the sons of God. **For the creation was subjected to futility, not willingly, but because of Him who subjected it, in hope** that the creation itself will be set free from its bondage to corruption and obtain the freedom of the glory of the children of God. (Rom. 8:18-21, emp. added)

Because Adam introduced sin into this world, God placed a curse on the universe. The curse involved most everything that still brings suffering[6] and emotional pain today: earthquakes, hurricanes, cancer, Alzheimer's, tornados, Autism, mosquito bites, floods, etc. God put the natural world under a curse so that the physical horrors of that curse – disease, famine, death – would become vivid pictures of the terror of sin. Dwelling in physical bodies, blind to anything beyond this material world, we need to see temporal suffering in order to begin to imagine the enormity of moral sin against an eternal Creator.

> *God put the natural world under a curse so that the physical horrors of that curse — disease, famine, death — would become vivid pictures of the terror of sin.*

Most kinds of suffering, from the smallest common cold to the loss of a parent due to the monster of cancer, serves as a billboard reminding us of the horrors of sin. We must remember that all suffering is not necessarily the result of our own *personal* sin. But ultimately, all suffering is at least a result of *Adam's* sin (cf. Gen. 3:14-24). Sin – Adam's sin, our neighbor's sin, or our own sin – is always the root cause of the world's suffering, either directly or indirectly. Whenever we are overcome with pain and suffering, it should drive us to hate sin all the more.

---

6 The argument can be made that perhaps Adam & Eve had the capicity to feel some sort of pain before the Fall, such as the pain one feels when he stubs his toe or touches a hot object. This is good pain; the body is alerting itself to danger. But the pre-Fall world is so foreign and distant to us, with the Bible giving little discription of it, that perhaps Adam & Eve were kept from any kind of harm. I do not know at what point the line is drawn regarding this point.

THIRD, SUFFERING ALLOWS CHRISTIANS TO DISPLAY THE GOD-HONORING TRUTH THAT CHRIST IS MORE PRECIOUS THAN ANYTHING IN THIS TEMPORAL WORLD THAT CAN BE LOST.

We live in a world full of loss – loss of comfort, loss of health, loss of property, and loss of life. This loss is intended to remind us of the horrors of sin. When you experience loss, you have two options: (a) you can murmur against God, or (b) you can hate sin.

> *When you murmur, you are communicating that God is not better than what you may have lost.*

There is a difference between *mourning* and *murmuring*. Murmuring is a great sin (Phil. 2:14; Jas. 5:9; Jude 16; 1 Cor. 10:10). To murmur is to grumble and whine, forgetting that everything we have in this life is in the context of God's blessings and provisions. In Jesus' parable of the laborers in the vineyard, some laborers murmured against the master because other laborers had received equal pay for less work (Matt. 20:1-16). The Israelites murmured against God because their journey to the Promised Land was sometimes difficult (Num. 14:1-3; Ex. 16:3). The Jews murmured because they did not believe Jesus when He told them He was "the bread that came down from heaven" (John 6:41-43). When people today disagree with God's terms of salvation, they are guilty of murmuring (Rom. 9:20).

When you experience loss, how will *you* react? Suffering gives us the perfect opportunity to demonstrate that God is more precious than anything you could have lost.

> Though the fig tree should not blossom,
> nor fruit be on the vines,
> the produce of the olive fail
> and the fields yield no food,
> the flock be cut off from the fold
> and there be no herd in the stalls,
> yet I will rejoice in the Lord;
> I will take joy in the God of my salvation. (Hab. 3:17-18)

One reason famine exists is so lovers of God can demonstrate that God is better than food. One reason disease and loss of our faculties exists is so Christians can demonstrate that a relationship with Jesus is better than health. One reason persecution exists is so Christians can demonstrate that a relationship with Jesus is better than physical safety.

Murmuring is a great sin. When you murmur, you are communicating that God is not better than what you may have lost. Murmuring is a reflection on God because it suggests that He should have given us more than He already has.

> Do all things without grumbling or disputing, that you may be blameless and innocent, children of God without blemish in the midst of a crooked and twisted generation, among whom you shine as lights in the world (Phil. 2:14-15)

HOPE IN CHRIST

If there was no pain, Jesus could not have felt pain (Isa. 53:3-5). If there was no suffering in this world, Jesus could not have suffered when He made Himself in the form of a human (Phil. 2:6-7). If there was no death, Jesus could not have experienced death (Phil. 2:8). And if there was no pain, suffering, and death, then God could not have demonstrated so clearly His love for us (Rom. 5:8). And now, God the Son, who experienced grief and sorrow like we do today, sits at the right hand of God (Rom. 8:34). Therefore, we do not have to think that God is somehow distant and detached from the suffering we experience in this world. The God who subjected creation to futility is the same God who entered this creation to experience that suffering on our behalf.

CONCLUSION

Just because God does not cause our immediate personal suffering does not mean He cannot use our suffering for His glory. Perhaps the bedrock truth of the book of Job is this: *Job didn't know*. He did not know about the conversation between God and Satan; He did not know why he lost his family; he did not know why he lost his health. Instead of finding clear reasons for why he was suffering, Job was left with God saying, in essence, "Trust me." In our confusion, we are reminded of Solomon's wise words, "As you do not know the way the spirit comes to the bones in the womb of a woman with child, so you do not know the work of God who makes everything" (Ecc. 11:5).

DISCUSSION QUESTIONS

1. Why is the so-called "problem of pain" a paradox and not a reason to disbelieve in God?

2. What is the difference between *evil* and *suffering*?

3. Does suffering prove there is no God? Why or why not?

4. Does suffering prove God is not in control? Why or why not?

5. Does suffering prove God is not all-loving? Why or why not?

6. Does suffering prove God is evil? Why or why not?

7. Is suffering always punishment for sin? Why or why not?

8. Is God always the direct cause behind all suffering?

9. What are some reasons why people suffer?

10. How can God use suffering for good?

CHAPTER 8

HOW DOES GOD WORK IN THE WORLD TODAY?

PROVIDENCE

OCCASIONALLY you will find a passage in the Bible that is so clear – so direct – so concise – that there is no getting around the implications today. Romans 8:28 is one such passage:

> And we know that for those who love God all things work together for good, for those who are called according to His purpose.

Paul's conviction needs to impress us. He does not say, "I sure hope everything will turn out okay in the end." He does not say, "I'm pretty sure things will work out." He writes, "We *know...*" All Christians should be comforted by this verse.

This begs the question: *how* does God work today? How exactly do "all things work together for good" for Christians? The answer can be found in a study of God's providence.

There is sometimes a lack of balance among the church today regarding the topic of providence. In my observation, some brethren are very committed to the reality of God's providence, whereas others hardly believe in it at all in any practical way. One way our western, pluralistic culture has infiltrated the church is through the pagan worldview that says that God is entirely isolated from creation, which is the false teaching of **deism** (see page 120). As a result, many Christians assume that because the natural world operates according to fixed natural laws with such regularity, God does not – and cannot – intervene in the world today. To these people, God is just a bystander in heaven looking down, perhaps occasionally 'cheering' for those who may be on His side. However, faithful followers of God in both the Old and New Testaments have always recognized God's hand in the world's affairs. That is what Paul said in Romans 8:28, communicating to us his full confidence in God's providence in the world today.

THE DEFINITION OF GOD'S PROVIDENCE

The word *providence* as we use it today does not occur in our English Bibles. It is just a word man uses to describe how God operates in His creation. However, God's providential hand can be seen throughout the pages of Scripture. Though the word may not be used, the *doctrine* of God's providence is there. Simply stated, providence is the means by which God *provides* for His creation. Or, as the late A.H. Strong writes:

> Providence is that continuous agency of God by which He makes all the events of the physical and moral universe fulfill the original design with which He created it.[1]

The term originally comes from the Latin word *providentia*, meaning "foresight" or "precaution," and the Greek word *pronoia* (used in Acts 24:2 and Romans 13:14), meaning "forethought" or "provision." For God to effectively care for the world, in His omniscience He must know the future and in His omnipotence ensure His Will is accomplished. Thus, in the words of Jack Cottrell:

> By "providence" we mean God's continuous activity of preserving and governing the universe by His knowledge, power, wisdom, and goodness, for the fulfillment of His purposes in creation.[2]

God's omnipotence is His *ability* to rule the world, His sovereignty is His *right* to rule the world, and His providence is the *means* by which He rules the world.

---

1 A.H. Strong, *Systematic Theology*, p. 418
2 Jack Cottrell, *The Faith Once for All*, p. 111

FOUNDATIONS TO PROPERLY UNDERSTANDING GOD'S PROVIDENCE

We see God's providence in Ephesians 4:6, where Paul says, "There is […] one God and Father of all, who is over all and through all and in all." Appreciating the following three traits as seen in Ephesians 4:6 is essential to properly understanding God's providence.

First, God is transcendent and in control of all things ("over all"). When we say that God is *transcendent*, we mean He exists above and independent to His creation. We are finite; He is infinite. His holiness and righteousness are beyond us. While all things are upheld by His mighty power (Heb. 1:3), He is upheld by no one. The whole universe exists in Him and for Him so that He will be honored, glorified, and praised. "For as the heavens are higher than the earth, so are my ways higher than your ways and my thoughts than your thoughts" (Isa. 55:9).

> *God's omnipotence is His **ability** to rule the world, His sovereignty is His **right** to rule the world, and His providence is the **means** by which He rules the world.*

Second, God is immanent in the world ("through all"). While distinct from His creation, God is also thoroughly present *in it*. In other words, there is no place where God is absent. Closely related to God's *immanence* is His omnipresence (but *immanence* goes one step further). God's *immanence* in His creation implies a deep, intimate relationship between Him and His creation. Not only is God actively present everywhere (omnipresence), but also "by Him all things consist" (Col. 1:17). If God is not immanent, all things would cease to be. W.T. Purkiser writes:

> Just as an artist is "outside" his work and "in" it, God is both superior to His universe and involved in its processes. God is transcendent as Creator. He is immanent as Sustainer.[3]

---

3 W.T. Purkiser, *Exploring Our Christian Faith*, p. 136

Third, God is preserving nature and its processes ("in all"). God is still working, even now, to uphold creation. If God were not active in the preservation of creation, then nature would necessarily be self-sustaining and self-perpetuating. Not only is this view unscientific, but it is also a doctrine foreign to the Bible. Jesus said, "My Father is working until now, and I am working" (John 5:17). The reason the universe continues to exist and function the way it does is because God is continually exerting His will to preserve it.

ANTI-PROVIDENCE VIEWS

Without understanding God's transcendence, immanence, and preservation of nature, you will eventually adopt a view of God's providence in the world that is thoroughly *unbiblical*. We will briefly examine the six most common misunderstandings below.

ATHEISM: "THERE IS NO GOD."

Atheism is the declaration that God does not exist. Closely akin to atheism is agnosticism, which is the intentional *doubting* of God's existence. Neither the atheist nor the agnostic believes God works in the world because they have chosen to disbelieve or doubt the reality of a Creator and Sustainer of the Universe.

CALVINISM: "GOD HAS *EVERYTHING* TO DO WITH EVERYTHING."

This view is the *opposite* of **atheism** and **secularism**. It holds that God is the *only* cause behind *everything* in the universe; that everything that has ever happened or will happen is dependent upon God. This is called **divine determinism**, which is the Calvinist doctrine of predestination. In other words, every event in history follows a sort of divine blueprint or computer program. Many Calvinists don't like how severe (and unscriptural) their view sounds, so they attempt to soften it by claiming that a person is still free when he follows the true desires of his heart. While this may sound like true freedom at first, we must remember that **Calvinism** also teaches that God has predetermined the desires of every man's heart. Thus we have gone full circle. Ultimately, this view claims that God predetermines *everything*, either by pre-programming our desires and motives, or by orchestrating everything directly. Providence, therefore, is simply the ongoing causation of everything He has eternally decreed will happen. We should praise God this view is false.

SECULARISM: "GOD HAS *NOTHING* TO DO WITH ANYTHING."

This view completely ignores God altogether and attributes every event in the world either to mankind or some kind of metaphysical natural law. Those who believe in karma or fate hold to this view. It is implied in popular phrases like, "Whatever will be, will be" ("Que sera, sera!") and "When your time is up, you're

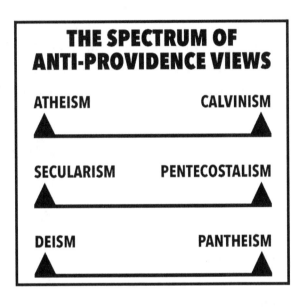

gonna go." Others claim that the laws of nature cause everything, including our own thoughts and choices. This is a secular form of **determinism**, meaning there is no such thing as free choice. Whatever form this view takes, it is ultimately the view that the world operates totally independent of God.

PENTECOSTALISM: "NOTHING IS PROVIDENTIAL; EVERYTHING IS MIRACULOUS."

The opposite of secularism is **Pentecostalism**. Those who hold this view not only affirm the reality of God's work in the world, but they go to the extreme of interpreting *everything* as a miracle. "A woman gave birth – it's a miracle!" "You recovered from a serious illness – it's a miracle!" "You made it through the line as the U.S. Post Office in less than 5 minutes – it must be a miracle!" (Well, I would agree with that one.) People who affirm this position believe that God works miracles every day. Not only do they confuse the difference between the natural and the supernatural, they also fail to recognize the very unique purpose of miracles. While the Lord (a) created the universe through miracles (cf. Gen. 1; Psa. 33:9), and (b) revealed His Will and validated its authenticity through miracles (cf. Ex. 24:1-9; Mark 16:20; Heb. 2:2-4), miracles are not being performed today. The Lord has ceased creating new matter (cf. Gen. 2:1-3), and He has ceased giving new revelation and confirming it miraculously (i.e. Scripture has been completed, 1 Cor. 13:8-13; Eph. 4:8-16; cf. John 20:30-31; Rom. 10:17).

DEISM: "GOD CREATED THE UNIVERSE THEN WALKED AWAY."

Deism has a purely naturalistic view of God's existence. While theism (the view found in Scripture) acknowledges God's eminence and providence in the world, deism totally removes God from *any* interaction with His creation. James Sire defines deism as the view that "a transcendent God, as a First Cause, created the universe but then left it to run on its own. God is thus not immanent, not fully personal, not sovereign over human affairs, not providential."[4] This view suggests that God created the universe like a clockmaker might build and wind a clock, never touching it again and allowing it to continue free from interruption.

PANTHEISM: "THERE IS NO CREATION IN WHICH SOME SORT OF GOD CAN OPERATE."

If the opposite of atheism is Calvinism, then the opposite of deism is **pantheism**. Deists believe the universe is totally separate from God,

---

4 James Sire, *The Universe Next Door*, p. 44

and pantheists believe the universe is totally one and the same as God. To the pantheist, it is logically impossible for a God to work in the universe because the universe *is* God, and God *is* the universe. The word is derived from a combination of the Greek word *pan*, meaning "all, everything," and *theos*, meaning "god, divine." Thus, pantheists believe that all is God and God is all. A cat is God, a tree is God, the sun is God, the clouds are God, you yourself are God, etc. In other words, the idea of God must never be separated from the universe. Pantheists hold that God is not the maker of the universe, but that He is the universe in its *totality*. Pantheism denies the transcendence of God. Different religions today hold to varying degrees of pantheism, including Hinduism, Buddhism, and the modern "New Age" movement.

FORMS OF PROVIDENCE

We will now look at different forms of God's providence so we can speak about God with greater precision.

GOD'S NATURAL PROVIDENCE

Because God is rational and orderly, He generally acts in a consistent manner. Nature is predictable for the most part. A pilot can calmly steer an 875,000-pound chunk of metal (a Boeing 747) down a short strip of pavement going 200 miles per hour because he is confident the laws of thermodynamics will give his aircraft flight. A farmer can invest thousands of dollars into fertilizer, seed, and machinery because he is confident his crop will yield 30- or 60- or 100-fold. A man knows to never ask a woman if she is pregnant[5] because he is confident she will smack him if he is wrong. The divine source of nature's regularity is implied in God's promise to Noah: "While the earth remains, seedtime and harvest, cold and heat, summer and winter, day and night, shall not cease" (Gen. 8:22).

---

5 Men, the exact rule is never never never never never never NEVER ask a woman if she is pregnant. Even if you are right, you will still be wrong every time. It is a law of nature.

As mentioned earlier, creation is dependent on a transcendent, immanent God. "In Him we live and move and have our being" (Acts 17:28; cf. Col. 1:17; Heb. 1:3). Thus, God's natural providence is *permissive*. This means that our undetermined free-will choices — and everything that happens in nature with unaided natural laws — are allowed to happen by God's *permission*.

Special providence is when God intervenes in the natural processes of nature. However, special providence is different from miraculous providence in that it does not involve suspending or overriding the way nature normally functions.

From a temporal point of view, God is the source and sustainer of nature. "He makes His sun rise on the evil and on the good, and sends rain on the just and on the unjust" (Matt. 5:45). Everything in nature is the work of God, whether the action is spontaneous or a process. God is no less the source of ripe grapes on a vine than He is the source of fruit of the vine miraculously appearing in in water pots (cf. John 2:1-11). But because of the familiarity and regularity of ripening grapes, we distinguish between the typical production of grape juice as being "natural," and the immediate, supernatural production of grape juice as being "miraculous."

GOD'S SPECIAL PROVIDENCE

God's special providence is the means of God's *purposeful* will, and not just His *permissive* will as expressed through natural providence. Special providence is when God intervenes in the natural processes of nature. However, special providence is different from miraculous providence in that it does not involve suspending or overriding the way nature normally functions. Jack Cottrell writes,

> In special providence God does manipulate natural law and influence free will choices, but He does not suspend or negate them. He thus causes results that would not have occurred without such intervention but which are still within the possibilities of natural law itself and

which do not violate the integrity of free will.[6]

Bear in mind that because of God's *general providence*, the natural world is orderly and predictable. Yet our immanent God so indwells His creation that He can intervene and change nature's intricate processes at His pleasure. God's *special providence* produces results that would not have otherwise happened under His *general providence*. The difference between God's *special* and *miraculous providence* is that God's special providence operates within the boundaries of nature, whereas God's miraculous providence circumvents the way which nature normally functions. We will now look at some ways in which God somehow intervenes in the world today by means of His *special providence*.

Much of the Old Testament, along with the accounts of the life and death of Jesus in the New Testament, is a record of God's providence in His scheme of redemption through Israel's history. The account of Joseph's life, for example, is a story of divine providence from beginning to end (cf. Gen. 45:4-8; 50:19-20). In another example, the account of Esther demonstrates how God used her to save His people (cf. Est. 4:14). During the Patriarchal Age, God sometimes required major decisions to be made by casting lots and allowing Him to determine how they fell (cf. Prov. 16:33). Time and time again, God determined the outcomes of Israel's military battles, sometimes against almost impossible odds (cf. Josh. 23:9; Judg. 3:28; 1 Sam. 23:4; 28:19; Isa 10:5, 15-16).

The Bible lists several ways in which God providentially operates so as to accomplish His ultimate will. God determines who will live and who will die (1 Sam. 2:6; 2 Sam. 12:18; Job 34:14-15; Jas. 4:15). By influencing individuals He controls the nations (cf. Josh. 23:9; Rom. 13:1; Hab. 1:6). He appoints the rulers of the earth (Job 34:24; Psa 75:7; Dan. 2:21) and shapes their judgments. "The king's heart is a stream of water in the hand of the Lord; He turns it wherever He will" (Prov. 21:1). He knows the outcome of events and thus uses

---

6 Jack Cottrell, *The Faith Once For All*, p. 121

every event – even sinful human decisions meant for evil – to carry out His good, *redemptive* purposes (Gen. 50:20; Acts 2:23; 4:27-28; Rom. 8:28). And He affects the disposition of people to give them a greater propensity for good or evil choices (1 Sam. 26:19; 2 Sam. 24:1; 1 Chron. 5:26; 2 Chron. 21:16; Ezra 1:1, 5; 6:22; 7:27).

How exactly does God providentially influence the actions and decisions of people without violating their free will? Calvinism asserts that mankind does not, technically, have any true ability to make free choices. Instead, according to Calvinism, everything is predetermined by God's decree. However, we reject Calvinism because this view is inconsistent with the teachings of Bible. Throughout Scripture, we find a loving, gracious God who asks man to love and follow Him out of his own volition.

Yet we are still left with one of the biggest, most complicated questions we can ever ask about God: How does God still accomplish His will today without violating mankind's freedom of choice?

I don't know.

Remember: A good theologian, or student of the Bible, is not someone who has everything figured out about God. Sometimes even the best students of the Bible must simply declare, "I don't know," from time to time. The best theologians simply take God at His Word, even if they can't quite fathom the *deeper* things of God, like how exactly God's providence works in every situation. I know God intervenes providentially in the world because the Bible tells me so, and in the next few paragraphs we will look at some ways in which He specifically works. I just don't always understand *how*. Yet despite my limited understanding, we know God is still actively controlling the course of the world affairs without violating mankind's ability to *choose*. If this subject does not motivate you to tremble before our Awesome God, nothing will.

First, we know God can influence human decisions by subtly altering the processes of nature. By nature, we are referring to every aspect of God's created order, including the weather, human biology, and the animal kingdom.

Surely one way God alters the processes of nature is by manipulating the weather. One can imagine all the ways humans can be affected by God sending "a great wind upon the sea" (Jonah 1:4), telling snow to "fall on the earth" (Job 37:6), and guiding storms to specific regions (Job 37:12-13). Obviously, by controlling the weather God can providentially control the nations (Job 36:31-33). All of us can think of ways our lives have been affected by adverse weather conditions (e.g. getting "snowed in," having a car hydroplane out of control, experiencing a power-outage, drought, etc.).

Surely another way God alters the normal processes of nature is by controlling our bodies and determining whether our immune systems will overcome sickness. For example, using the nervous system, God can influence our arm and finger muscles to subtly change the outcome of certain events (1 Kings 22:34; Prov. 16:33; cf. Jonah 1:7; Acts 1:26). As another example, God can alter the chemical balance in the brain to cause irrational behavior (Dan. 4:33; 6:22). He can also boost the body's immune system to naturally fight off a disease (cf. Isa. 38:1-5; Jas. 5:14-16) as well as weaken the immune system, causing one to succumb to disease and death (2 Sam. 12:14-18; 2 Chron. 21:14-19; Amos 4:10).

Yet another way God's providence works through nature is by controlling the animal kingdom. "The young lions roar for their prey, seeking their food from God" (Psa. 104:21). "He gives to the beasts their food, and to the young ravens that cry" (Psa. 147:9). The animals "neither sow nor reap nor gather into barns, and yet your heavenly Father feeds them" (Matt. 6:25-33). Nothing happens in the animal world – not even the death of a bird – apart from the providential allowance of God (Matt. 10:29). Not only does God provide for the animal world, but historically has also used the animal world to accomplish His will. For example, God sent every kind of animal into Noah's ark (Gen. 7:2-3); He providentially ensured that a ram would be "caught in a thicket by his horns" at the same time and place Abraham was about to sacrifice Isaac (Gen. 22:13); He caused a plant to quickly grow over Jonah's head to provide shade (Jon. 4:6); He filled Egypt with frogs (Ex. 8:6), gnats (Ex. 8:16), flies (Gen. 8:24), plague (Ex. 9:6), and locusts (Ex. 10:13-15) as divine punishment to Pharaoh; He sent quails into the camp of Israel (Num. 11:31; Psa. 78:25-29; 105:40); He caused ravens to bring bread and meat to Elijah during the famine (1 Kings 17:6); He sent fiery serpents to bite and punish Israel (Num. 21:6); He used a lion to kill a disobedient prophet (1 Kings 13:24-26); He shut the lions' mouths to protect Daniel (Dan. 6:22).

God can do all of this – influencing the weather, our bodies, and animal life – without using miracles. Much of God's providential work can be explained using natural events.

Second, God can influence human decisions by manipulating a *series* of natural events. God can so orchestrate events that they produce outcomes that will ultimately accomplish His Will and the welfare of His children (Rom. 8:28). He knows every human being so intimately well that He can alter circumstances around us in the *perfect* way, foreknowing our different reactions.

Naturally, even without God's providential involvement, there are thousands of variables that affect your behavior and your decisions every day. Thus, we should not be so naïve as to think that God does not, at least occasionally, manipulate daily circumstances so as to accomplish His will (and to work for the ultimate *good* of Christians). God has every right to change the outcome of personal decisions. Paul wrote:

> Has the potter no right over the clay, to make out of the same lump one vessel for honorable use and another for dishonorable use? What if God, desiring to show His wrath and to make known His power, has endured with much patience vessels of wrath prepared for destruction, in order to make known the riches of His glory for vessels of mercy, which He has prepared beforehand for glory — even us whom He has called, not from the Jews only but also from the

Gentiles? (Rom. 9:21-24).

We must go out of our way to remind ourselves, however, that God will never *coerce* someone to commit sin. God does not tempt people (Jas. 1:13); rather, people are enticed by their our own desires and attitudes (Jas. 1:14). At the same time, God can so perfectly orchestrate events that even wicked people — once they have already decided to do evil — end up accomplishing His Will. God used even the hardened Pharoah to bring God glory. But it must be stressed that it is the individual's fault – not God's – for allowing one's heart to harden (Heb. 3:8).

We should also note that sometimes God's special providence does not have the desired effect (cf. Amos 4:6-11; Hag. 1:1-11). Why? To demonstrate that men are without excuse and are ultimately responsible for their own choices (cf. Rom. 1:20).

GOD'S MIRACULOUS PROVIDENCE

In God's **general providence**, God *permits* the laws of nature to function normally and free-will choices to be made unimpeded. In God's **special providence**, God *purposefully intervenes* by influencing the free-will choices of man in natural ways. In God's **miraculous providence** (or, just "miracles"), God *bypasses* the way things naturally happen to produce a desired result.

There is an implicit fallacy in saying that a miracle "violates" the laws of nature, as God does not violate His own laws. God is actively sustaining the natural laws of nature, and a miracle happens when God temporarily suspends the way nature normally functions. Unlike God's special providence, which acts in *harmony* with natural law, God's miraculous providence works *differently* than natural law. In other words, a miracle cannot be explained by natural law alone. Even the enemies of Christianity could not explain away the miracles worked by the apostles of Jesus (cf. Acts 4:14-16).

We will talk more about miracles in a future *You Are A Theologian* volume. But for now, we agree with the words of W.T. Purkiser:

> The willingness and ability of God to act in ways that are out of the ordinary pattern of nature add richness to the doctrine of providence, and reveal God more in the capacity of Heavenly Father than as an austere First Cause.[7]

PRINCIPLES FOR UNDERSTANDING GOD'S PROVIDENCE

It is very important that we understand the following principles regarding God's providence. Any understanding of providence needs to be in harmony with God's Word.

First, God will never providentially operate in a way that is contrary to His nature or His Word. God is holy (Lev. 19:2) and righteous (Psa. 145:17), and therefore will not providentially operate in a way that is inconsistent with His being. While God may manipulate nature and orchestrate events, He will never tempt people to do evil (Jas. 1:13-14).

Second, God will never providentially operate in a way that violates man's freedom of choice. Contrary to the teachings of Calvin, Augustine, and Zwingli (all of whom taught that mankind is unable to *choose* to do righteousness), the Bible teaches that man is free to choose whether to obey or disobey God (cf. Josh. 24:15; Matt. 23:37; John 5:39-40; Rev. 2:5, 16, 21-22; 3:3, 19; 22:17). Therefore, God will not force someone to choose to do right or wrong. God is no respecter of persons (Acts 10:34-35), and will not nebulously ordain that some obey Him while coercing others to disobey Him. He can, however, override the outcome of someone's evil decision and use it for good.

For example, God used the murderous intentions of Joseph's brothers to deliver Israel (Gen. 50:19-20). God used the greedy slave-owners who threw Paul and Silas in prison to bring the gospel to

---

7 W.T. Purkiser, *Exploring Our Christian Faith*, p. 138

that region (1 Thess. 2:1-2). God orchestrated the cowardly, corrupt Pilate, the evil Jewish leaders, and the crooked Judas to bring about the crucifixion of Jesus, resulting in the gift of salvation to the whole world (Acts 5:30-31). God used the martyrdom of Stephen in Acts 7 to cause a widespread dispersion of Christians into the world to further spread the gospel (Acts 8:1).

Third, God's special providence must be distinguished from God's miracles. God's *miracles* (a) are observable and quantifiable, (b) supersede natural law, and (c) teach an underlying truth. God's *special providence*, on the other hand, does not fit into any of these categories. Miracles are observable and quantifiable in that they can be seen and distinguished from natural events, such as a resurrection from the dead (John 11:43-44), floating disembodied fingers writing on walls (Dan. 5:5), and a dozen baskets of leftover food (John 6:13). Such examples are all undeniably supernatural events. Miracles supersede natural law in that they cannot be explained by natural phenomena. Additionally, miracles teach an underlying truth in that they are designed to elicit a faith response (e.g. Heb. 2:3-4). For instance, when Jesus healed a paralytic, He explained the reason why was so that we "may know that the Son of Man has authority on earth to forgive sins" (Mark 2:10).

Note an example of how God's *special providence* is different than God's *miracles*. First, note that when Mary was still a virgin she "was found to be with child from the Holy Spirit" (Matt. 1:18-25; Luke 1:30-37) - a fulfillment of Isaiah's prophecy (Isa 7:14). Mary's conception while still a virgin cannot be explained naturally, thus it was a miracle. On the other hand, Hannah, of the Old Testament, was unable to conceive because her womb had been "closed" (1 Sam. 1:6). Yet she "prayed to the Lord and wept bitterly" (1 Sam. 1:10), promising the Lord that she would dedicate her son to His service if He would bless her with a son. God "remembered her," and her husband "knew Hannah his wife," and she "conceived and bore a son" (1 Sam. 1:19-20). Clearly, Hannah's conception can be explained by natural phenomena, whereas Mary's conception can only be a miracle.

Fourth, God's special providence is not usually easily discernable.
Without the Bible specifically telling us that God is at work in our lives, we would not know anything about God's providence. Even now, we may suspect that God is working providentially in our lives, but we may not be able to prove it. Mordecai was unsure whether God was using Esther to save the lives of the Jews, so he remarked, "Who knows whether you have not come to the kingdom for such a time as this?" (Est. 4:14). The apostle Paul, unsure whether God orchestrated his meeting with the runaway slave Onesimus, said in his letter to Onesimus' master, Philemon, "For this perhaps is why he was parted from you for a while, that you might have him back forever" (Phile. 15). If an inspired apostle was reluctant to claim something was an act of providence, we should be just as reluctant today. We know that God is at work behind the scenes (cf. Rom. 8:28), but we are frequently unaware of *how*, or even *if*, He is operating in a given circumstance.

> *If an inspired apostle was reluctant to claim something was an act of providence, we should be just as reluctant today. We know that God is at work behind the scenes, but we are frequently unaware of **how**, or even **if**, He is operating in a given circumstance.*

SOME PROMISES MADE TRUE THROUGH PROVIDENCE

God's providence guarantees several His promises that are precious to us.

1. THE BIBLE PRESERVED FOR US

We do not have to wonder whether the Word of God has been lost or distorted throughout the centuries. Jesus said, "Heaven and Earth will pass away, but my words will not pass away" (Matt. 24:35; Mark 13:31).

Men have tried in vain to destroy or alter the Bible. Our vast wealth of Old and New Testament manuscripts and the science of textual criticism have made it incredibly easy to pinpoint even the slightest variation in our copies of the ancient words. We should find great comfort in the fact that God has preserved His revelation to mankind, and we do not have to fear it ever being lost.

2. NO TEMPTATION TOO GREAT FOR US

Providence makes this promise sweet to every Christian:

> No temptation has overtaken you that is not common to man. God is faithful, and He will not let you be tempted beyond your ability, but with the temptation He will also provide the way of escape, that you may be able to endure it. (1 Cor. 10:13)

Do not be fooled; as long as you are living on this earth, you will face temptation. But God, in His providence, will ensure we do not face any temptation to sin that is too great to handle. The same God who understands our temptation (Heb. 4:15) will always provide a way of escape. Therefore, Christians, we must continue walking in the light (1 John 1:7)!

3. HARDSHIPS WORK IN OUR FAVOR

Only Christians are promised that "all things work together for good" (Rom. 8:28). Of course, this does not mean that *only* good will happen to us. Nor does it mean that everything will turn out for the best in this present life. What it does mean, however, is that "all things" – including tribulation, distress, persecution, famine, nakedness, peril, or sword (Rom. 8:35) – will ultimately work out in our favor and we will be "more than conquerors through Him who loved us" (Rom. 8:37). As we stand at the doorstep of eternity, we can only begin to fathom the richness of this promise.

4. OUR PRAYERS ANSWERED

Our prayers are only effective if God is working today in the world through His providence. Thankfully, He is working (John 5:17), and thus our prayers are working too. The Bible is full of promises that every Christian's prayer, if prayed properly, will be answered (e.g. Matt. 7:7-11; 21:22). "The prayer of a righteous person has great power as it is working" (Jas. 5:16). While God may not answer in the way we desire, He does promise to answer our prayers in the best way possible (cf. Matt. 7:9). God's provision is always sufficient for us (2 Cor. 12:9), even if we do not understand His answers presently. But we can always rely on our heavenly Father to provide from the standpoint of His love for us and His infinite foreknowledge. Cecil May, Jr. writes,

> Jesus taught us to pray, "Your will be done, on earth as it is in heaven" (Matt. 6:10). To pray for God's will to be done is to pray for the best possible outcome. As in Jesus' case (cf. Luke 22:42), it may not seem good for the moment, but its culmination is victory. Thursday night was despair in the garden. Friday night was death and burial. But Sunday came with resurrection and triumph. In the dark times, what seems to be defeat and despair, we should be faithful, keep on loving God, and keep praying.[8]

CONCLUSION

Paul reminds fathers, "If anyone does not provide for his relatives, and especially for members of his household, he has denied the faith and is worse than an unbeliever" (1 Tim. 5:8). It is the responsibility of each head of the household to make provision for the needs of his family; that is, he must anticipate the essentials of life and then meet those needs. If this is true for earthly fathers, how much more true is it of our heavenly Father? Christians are part of a great "household of faith" (Gal. 6:10; Eph. 2:19), and as such, we have a Great Father who provides (Mal. 2:10; Matt. 23:9; 1 Cor. 8:6; Eph. 4:6; 1 Pet. 1:3). When Jesus said, "Do not be anxious about your life, what you will eat

---

8 Cecil May, Jr., *Providence*, p. 50

or what you will drink, nor about your body, what you put on" (Matt. 6:25), He was not telling us to live carelessly; He was telling us we can rely on the providence of God. Therefore, we must live confidently in Him.

Throughout life's hardships, we cling to Paul's words, "For those who love God all things work together for good, for those who are called according to His purpose" (Rom. 8:28). Hardships may come, but they cannot separate us from the love of Christ and eternity with Him (Rom. 8:37-38).

DISCUSSION QUESTIONS

1. Why do you think Christians are sometimes reluctant to acknowledge God's providence in the world today?

2. In your own words, what does **providence** mean?

3. What three attributes are essential in properly understanding God's providence?

4. What are six anti-providence views today? How do they fit on a spectrum in relation to the Bible?

5. What is God's **general providence**?

6. What is God's **special providence**?

7. What is God's **miraculous providence**?

8. What are some principles that help us better understand God's providence?

9. Will God override your ability to make free moral choices?

10. What are some promises for Christians today that can be only be true if God is presently working in the world today?

CHAPTER 9

WHEN YOU DON'T DESIRE GOD

ENLARGING OUR LOVE FOR GOD

Jesus answered, "The most important is,
'Hear, O Israel: The Lord our God, the
Lord is one. And you shall love the Lord
your God with all your heart and with
all your soul and with all your mind and
with all your strength.'"
(Mark 12:29-30)

DO you love God with all of your heart, soul, mind, and strength? The question is not whether you want to, but whether you do already. The Bible is full of commands to *love – seek – hunger – thirst – crave – desire* God.

- "Oh, taste and see that the Lord is good! Blessed is the man who takes refuge in Him!" (Psa. 34:8)
- "Then I will go to the altar of God, to God my exceeding joy" (Psa. 43:4)
- "Restore to me the joy of your salvation, and uphold me with a willing spirit." (Psa. 51:12)
- "O God, you are my God; earnestly I seek you; my soul thirsts for you; my flesh faints for you, as in a dry and weary land where there is no water." (Psa. 63:1)
- "Satisfy us in the morning with your steadfast love, that we may rejoice and be glad all our days." (Psa. 90:14)
- "'The Lord is my portion,' says my soul, 'therefore I will hope in

Him.'" (Lam. 3:24)

- ▪ "If anyone has no love for the Lord, let him be accursed. Our Lord, come!" (1 Cor. 16:22)
- ▪ "Rejoice in the Lord always; again I will say, rejoice." (Phil. 4:4)

WHEN THERE IS NO DESIRE FOR GOD

But, upon seeing all the Biblical evidence that we are supposed to delight in God, some are honest enough to say, "I don't think I have ever felt that deep desire for God."

Why is it that we sometimes don't feel any discernible desire Him? Emotionally speaking, why are we sometimes numb to God's glory – to the point where we might even feel *indifferent* about the prospect of spending eternity with Him? Even some of our worship services, Bible classes, prayer meetings, lectureships, seminars, and fellowship gatherings in many of our churches – instead of being spiritually uplifting – have become emotionally draining.

WHERE SHOULD YOU BEGIN?

The Bible clearly teaches that if we are to please God, we need to obey Him from the heart. We are not to obey Him just because we feel *obligated* to obey Him, but because we actually *love* to obey Him (though obedience is certainly not *less* than obligation). Jesus says, "If you love me, you will keep my commandments" (John 14:15). Love should come first, followed by obedience. God has never been pleased with obedience out of cold, religious ritual. "This people honors me with their lips, but their heart is far from me" (Matt. 15:8).

Of course, if you are to desire God, you must first *want* to desire God. Like the father pleading with Jesus to heal his demon-possessed son, we cry, "I believe; help my unbelief!" (Mark 9:24). But you cannot simply decide to have a genuine, heartfelt desire for God, just as you can't just *decide* to start loving classical or country[1] music. If you want to start loving a new genre of music, something needs to change *inside of you* to make the music attractive and compelling to you. Likewise, to feel a true love for God, something must change inside of you. To experience this inner renewal of the spirit (cf. Eph. 4:23), you need to get to know God by studying and listening to His Word.

If you do not know Him, you cannot desire Him. You must open your heart and make yourself vulnerable to His will for your life. Pour yourself into the things He has said. God and His will for our lives is so potent that it is capable of "piercing to the division of soul and of spirit, of joints and of marrow, and discerning the thoughts and intentions of the heart" (Heb. 4:12). We must let the Potter mold us in such a way that we will desire Him from the heart (cf. Isa. 29:16; Rom. 9:21).

SIN, ETERNITY, AND THE FIGHT OF YOUR LIFE

Perhaps the biggest reason many do not desire God is because they do not truly believe their eternal life is really at stake. Paul urges us to "fight the good fight of faith. Take hold of the eternal life" (1 Tim. 6:12). This is war! We must fight to attain a desire for God! When we fight, God will fight with us and renew within us a zeal for Him.

> Therefore, my beloved, as you have always obeyed, so now, not only as in my presence but much more in my absence, work out your own salvation with fear and trembling, *for it is God who works in you, both to will and to work for His good pleasure.* (Phil. 2:12-13)

REMEMBER THE ENORMITY OF SIN

Have we forgotten what it is like to be separated from God? Our sins have separated us from Him (Isa. 59:1-2). Yet, because of God's pure goodness, He has offered to reestablish our relationship with Him. Or, as the apostle Paul says,

---

1 Actually, no sane person listens to country music.

> But God, being rich in mercy, because of the great love with which He loved us, even when we were dead in our trespasses, made us alive together with Christ—by grace you have been saved (Eph. 2:4-5).

If we are to desire God, we must realize how utterly unworthy of God we really are. We do not deserve heaven any more than the rich man deserved a drop of water on his tongue as he suffered in torment in the Hadean realm (cf. Luke 16:24). The disease of sin stains us and spreads over our vessels like cancer. We are powerless on our own in defeating sin. With Paul we cry, "Wretched man that I am! Who will deliver me from this body of death?" (Rom. 7:24).

We must recognize that even at our best, we are still "unworthy servants" (Luke 17:10). Only when we see ourselves in the light of God's glory will He extend His offer of a relationship with Him (cf. Isa. 6:5-7). There is no such thing as a prideful, arrogant Christian. "God opposes the proud, but gives grace to the humble" (Jas. 4:6). He only draws those who seek grace (John 6:43-45).

Only God can raise a dead man. If He can give flesh and life to a pile of dry bones (Eze. 37:3-6), and if He can make a camel pass through the eye of a needle (Matt. 19:24), then He can give life even to you. Like the tax collector in the temple of God, we simply need to know our humble place and say from the heart, "God, be merciful to me, a sinner!" (Luke 18:13-14).

SEEK GOD'S WILL OVER YOUR OWN

We were dead in our sins, and God raised us from the dead. But God didn't raise everything about us. When He saved us, He gave us a new identity. Paul explains it this way:

> It is no longer I who live, but Christ who lives in me. And the life I now live in the flesh I live by faith in the Son of God, who loved me and gave Himself for me. (Gal. 2:20)

Christians are people who are living someone else's life. We have died to ourselves (Luke 9:23-24); therefore we do not want the kinds of things that our former, dead, wretched selves wanted. We are to desire God's Will more than anything else. With Jesus we pray, "Our Father in heaven, [...] your Will be done, on earth as it is in heaven" (Matt. 6:10). Or with Samuel we say, "May the Lord do what seems good to Him" (2 Sam. 10:12).

When we start living to do God's *Will*, we will begin to desire *Him*. Like Jesus, we can truly say, "My food" – the very desires of my heart – "is to do the Will" of God (John 4:34). We were created to serve God (Ecc. 12:13) and to bring glory to Him (1 Cor. 10:31).

Ask yourself, "Am I truly living for Him?" If you are not living for Him, you are not doing what you were made to do. If you are looking for joy in materialism, wealth, sex, power, or fame, you will not find it. The Christian who lives his or her life in the pursuit of anything but God is experiencing an identity crisis.

If you truly want to desire God, you must be proactive in your pursuit of Him. Immerse yourself in the life you know God wants you to live. Cleanse out the leaven of sin (cf. 1 Cor. 5:7). Christ has made you dead to sin (Rom.

> *If you truly want to desire God, you must be proactive in your pursuit of Him.*

6:5-6); start living as though you are dead to sin (Rom. 6:11)! You have been made alive with Christ (Eph. 2:5); therefore start "seeking things that are above" (Col. 3:1)! You have been made holy in Christ (Col. 3:12); therefore "be holy in all your conduct" (1 Pet. 1:15)! You are the light of the world in Christ (Matt. 5:14); therefore let your light shine (Matt. 5:16)!

SPEND TIME WITH GOD'S WORD

If the devil could have just one victory, he would choose to keep you away from God's Word. It is a great sin to neglect the Bible. After all, you can never desire God if you are not consciously spending time meditating on the things He has said. Recognize the sinful inclination to minimize the regular study of His Word, and overcome this tendency. "Put to death therefore what is earthly in you," Paul says (Col. 3:5). Do not neglect your appointment with the Word. It is the Bible that gives us faith (Rom. 10:17), and by faith we have hope (Rom. 5:2). Paul says, "You received the Word [...] with the joy of the Holy Spirit" (1 Thess. 1:6). Being "filled with the Spirit," as Ephesians 5:18-19 commands, means letting "the Word of Christ dwell within you richly," as the parallel passage, Colossians 3:16, indicates.

THE WORD GIVES LIFE

Jesus came so that Christians can have an abundant life (John 10:10) – a life that desires God. After we have been given new life at the moment of baptism (John 3:5; 1 Pet. 3:21), the way in which we start realizing the abundant life is by the Word of God (1 Pet. 1:23-25). "The words that I have spoken to you," Jesus said, "are spirit and life" (John 6:63). The reason God gave us the Bible is so that we may "have life in His name" (John 20:31). We are to live by the words of God (Matt. 4:4).

Oh, how easy it is to be duped by the allures of materialism, thinking that we can find joy in *things*! It is the *Word* that gives us life (John 6:68). And the more we know God's Word, the more abundantly we can live our new life in Christ.

THE WORD GIVES US HOPE

God gave us Scripture in order to teach us, "and through the encouragement of the Scriptures we might have hope" (Rom. 15:4). If you do not find hope in God, perhaps it is because you are hoping in other things. God's Word is what has made known "the riches of the glory of this mystery, which is Christ in you, the hope of glory" (Col 1:27; cf. 1 Thess. 1:3; Tit. 2:13; Eph. 1:12).

THE WORD FREES US FROM THE SLAVERY OF SIN

Sin numbs us – defiles us – binds us – deceives us (Eph. 4:22). We become addicted to it (Phil. 3:19) and are left powerless as it pummels us (1 Pet. 2:11). Jesus taught that those who commit sin are slaves to sin (John 8:34).

God's Word frees us when we study it, meditate on it, and apply it (John 8:32). Sin defiles, but Scripture sanctifies (John 17:17). The more time we spend with the Word, the more pure we become. Listening to God gives us a pure heart (Matt. 5:8).

THE WORD OFFERS ANSWERS TO OUR PRAYERS

Jesus says, "If you abide in me, and my words abide in you, ask whatever you wish, and it will be done for you" (John 15:7). As we seek God's Will, we will want His Will to be accomplished above our own will. And when we pray, "if we ask anything according to His Will He hears us" (1 John 5:14).

THE WORD IS THE SOURCE OF WISDOM

The Bible reveals "all the treasures of wisdom and knowledge" (Col. 2:3). The more we are exposed to the Word of God and the last will and testament of Jesus, the more we see things as they really are. Paul writes,

> The natural person does not accept the things of the Spirit of God, for they are folly to him, and he is not able to understand them because they are spiritually discerned. The spiritual person judges all things, but is himself to be judged by no one. "For who has understood the mind of the Lord so as to instruct him?" But we have the mind of Christ. (1 Cor. 2:14-16)

THE WORD IS OUR WEAPON AGAINST THE DEVIL

Every time, Jesus responded to temptation with Scripture (Matt. 4:4, 7, 10). The Word is our weapon in our fight against the devil. Paul advises, "In all circumstances take up the shield of faith, with which you can extinguish all the flaming darts of the evil one" (Eph. 6:16). Peter commands, "Resist [the devil], stand firm in your faith" (1 Pet. 5:9). Where do we find faith? We find it in the Word (Rom. 10:17).

THE WORD IS OUR SOURCE OF JOY

Could it be that we do not desire God because we have not desired His Word? Perhaps we have fallen for the lie of much of today's contemporary religious literature that teaches we can feel a desire for God apart from a working knowledge of Scripture. Yet this is not what God has said in His Word. The psalmist declares:

> The Law of your mouth is better to me
> than thousands of gold and silver pieces. (Psa. 119:72)

> How sweet are your Words to my taste,
> sweeter than honey to my mouth! (Psa. 119:103)

> Therefore I love your commandments
> above gold, above fine gold. (Psa. 119:127)

> I rejoice at your Word
> like one who finds great spoil. (Psa. 119:162)

Job declares, "I have not departed from the commandment of His lips; I have treasured the words of His mouth more than my portion of food" (Job 23:12). Jeremiah says, "Your words were found, and I ate them, and your words became to me a joy and the delight of my heart" (Jer. 15:16). Can you relate to that? If not, the key to desiring God is to start indulging in the study of His words.

We need to make the Bible the very basis of everything we are. I love being around older faithful Christians, because they have spent so much time with God's Word that it has become who they are. The way they talk – the way they think – the advice they give – the decisions they make are so firmly grounded in Scripture that it makes me desire to have what they have. C.H. Spurgeon said it this way:

> It is blessed to eat into the very soul of the Bible until, at last, you come to talk in Scriptural language, and your very style is fashioned upon Scripture models, and, what is better still, your spirit is flavored with the words of the Lord. [...] Prick [the man of God] anywhere—his blood is Bibline, the very essence of the Bible flows from him. He cannot speak without quoting a text, for his very soul is full of the Word of God.[2]

SIT AT THE FEET OF GREAT TEACHERS

Today, most of the cheap promises of "spiritual growth" are made by self-help devotional books and easy-to-read how-to books. In reality, seldom does one cultivate a desire for God when he or she thinks spiritual blessings will fall so easily onto one's lap. Do not be lazy or passive in looking for great truths about God's Word. Listen to the advice of the wise father:

> My son, if you receive my words and treasure up my commandments with you, making your ear attentive to wisdom and inclining your heart to understanding; yes, if you call out for insight and raise your voice for understanding, if you seek it like silver and search for it as for hidden treasures, then you will understand the fear of the Lord and find the knowledge of God. For the Lord gives wisdom; from His mouth come knowledge and understanding; (Prov. 2:1-6)

You must be active in your pursuit of the understanding of God's Word. If you do not sit at the feet of wise, knowledgeable Christians, you will not unlock the depth of God's wisdom.

Fill your bookshelf with rich theological books. Have captivating theological conversations with older Christians. Attend church lectureships and study theological issues. C.S. Lewis wrote, "For my own part, I tend to find the doctrinal books often more helpful in

---

2 Spurgeon, C. H. *Autobiography*, p. 268

devotion than the devotional books, and I rather suspect that the same experience may await many others."[3]

Of course, meaty books filled with bad theology will suck you dry of any spiritual joy just as much as any bad devotional book will. But don't stop eating steak just because your last bite had too much gristle. Some of the great works in Christian theology are old. Read books by great Christians of the past, such as Moses Lard, J.W. McGarvey, Alexander Campbell, David Lipscomb, Guy N. Woods, Robert Milligan, N.B. Hardeman, Rex Turner, Gus Nichols, Franklin Camp, and Thomas B. Warren.

EMBRACE THE PEOPLE OF THE BOOK

Make sure your closest of friends are strong Christians. You were never meant to walk with God alone. Paul said, "We work with you for your joy" (2 Cor. 1:24). "Exhort one another every day" (Heb. 3:12-13). "Whoever walks with the wise becomes wise" (Prov. 13:20). "Stir up one another to love and good works" (Heb. 10:24-25). *Christianity is relational.*

Whenever someone tells me they feel stagnant in their faith, one of the first things I ask is whether they regularly attend all the worship assemblies of the church and are actively involved day-to-day with other Christians. Their answer is usually no.

If you want to desire God, you must spend time with His children. The way to the Father is through the Son (John 14:6), and Jesus said that "whoever does the Will of God, he is my brother and sister and mother" (Mark 3:35). All faithful Christians are His children (Rom. 8:17). Thus it is impossible to experience any real joy in God without being an active member of His family.

God wants us to view our identity as members of a larger body. Paul writes,

---

3 C.S. Lewis, *God In The Dock*, p. 205

> For just as the body is one and has many members, and all the members of the body, though many, are one body, so it is with Christ. [...] For the body does not consist of one member but of many. If the foot should say, "Because I am not a hand, I do not belong to the body," that would not make it any less a part of the body. [...] But God has so composed the body, giving greater honor to the part that lacked it, that there may be no division in the body, but that the members may have the same care for one another. If one member suffers, all suffer together; if one member is honored, all rejoice together. (1 Cor. 12:12, 14-15, 24-26)

You can't be a Christian without being connected to a local body of believers. In fact, you need to be vying for the title, "Most Active Church Member." This is why God speaks of the rare time a member needs to be removed from the local church:

> For what have I to do with judging outsiders? Is it not those inside the church whom you are to judge? God judges those outside. 'Purge the evil person from among you.' (1 Cor. 5:12-13)

If Christians were not required by God to be a formal part of the church, then such a formal *removal* would not be possible.

I believe it is critically important to stress local church membership, due in part because this Biblical teaching goes against the grain of our individualistic culture. Today, people hold *accountability* and *obligation* in contempt. We tend to flee anything we feel might hold us back from pursuing whatever whim or fancy we happen to be craving that particular second. But God has designed the church to protect us from ourselves; He requires our brothers and sisters in Christ to protect us from anything that would steal our spiritual joy in God.

INVEST IN THE WORK OF GOD

Your heart becomes attached to the things in which you are invested. Is it any wonder that some of the happiest Christians are some of the most *giving* of Christians? We see this in 2 Corinthians 8:1-4, where Paul is celebrating the church in Macedonia for helping the church in Jerusalem.

We want you to know, brothers, about the grace of God that has been given among the churches of Macedonia, for in a severe test of affliction, their abundance of joy and their extreme poverty have overflowed in a wealth of generosity on their part. For they gave according to their means, as I can testify, and beyond their means, of their own accord, begging us earnestly for the favor of taking part in the relief of the saints—and this, not as we expected, but they gave themselves first to the Lord and then by the will of God to us. (2 Cor. 8:1-9)

God does not feel loved when we give grudgingly and unenthusiastically. How could He? When people reluctantly serve you, do you feel loved? Paul could not be clearer in what God expects of Christians: "Each one must give as he has decided in his heart, not reluctantly or under compulsion, for God loves a cheerful giver" (2 Cor. 9:7).

If you struggle having a desire to contribute to the church with your time, money, or energy, you must ask God to help you desire Him. "Satisfy us in the morning with your steadfast love, that we may rejoice and be glad all our days" (Psa. 90:14). "Restore to me the joy of your salvation, and uphold me with a willing spirit" (Psa. 51:12). "Will you not revive us again, that your people may rejoice in you?" (Psa. 85:6). We need to take Jesus' words to heart: "Ask, and you will receive, that your joy may be full" (John 16:24).

FIGHT AGAINST SIN

Sin slows us down and steals our joy in Christ. "Let us also lay aside every weight, and sin which clings so closely, and let us run with endurance the race that is set before us" (Heb. 12:1).

When facing our sins, we can do one of two things: We can excuse it, or we can expose it. If we are to grow in our desire for God, we must grow in our hatred of sin. We must take it seriously, kill it, hate it, stomp it out, and trust Jesus to deliver us from its power over us.

One of the reasons people do not feel a desire for God is because they are unwilling to expose whatever sin remains in their lives. Whatever sin you hold on to will eat away at you. David says,

> For when I kept silent, my bones wasted away through my groaning all day long. For day and night your hand was heavy upon me; my strength was dried up as by the heat of summer. I acknowledged my sin to you, and I did not cover my iniquity; I said, "I will confess my transgressions to the Lord," and you forgave the iniquity of my sin. (Psa. 32:3-5)

Both a sin against your brother (Matt. 5:23-24) and a sin against your spouse will smother your worship. But like David, if we confess our sin, we can experience the freedom of "the man against whom the Lord counts no iniquity" (Psa. 32:2).

If we repent of our sin, we do not have to endure God's wrath upon our consciences (Gal. 3:13; cf. 1 Pet. 3:21). When we confess our sin, Christ clothes us in His righteousness. "In Him we might become the righteousness of God" (2 Cor. 5:21). Don't just confess your sins in prayer to God – confess your sins to your brethren (Jas. 5:16).

CONCLUSION

Do you desire God, or do you feel distant from Him? Peter writes,

> Therefore, brothers, be all the more diligent to confirm your calling and election, for if you practice these qualities you will never fall. (2 Pet. 1:10)

Learn to desire God by listening to His Word, meditating on it and studying it. Spend time with people of the Book and sit at their feet. Make sure you are an active, supportive, and giving member of the body of Christ.

It is a great paradox: if you wish to grow in your desire for God, you must not focus too much on your actual desire. You must instead focus on the work of God.

DISCUSSION QUESTIONS

1. Why do you think God wants us to desire Him?

2. For what reason should we obey the commands of Jesus?

3. Can you simply decide to start desiring God? Why or why not?

4. Why does the Bible emphasize so much the reading, listening, and studying of the Word?

5. How does sin numb our desire for God?

6. Can you come to a deep familiarity with God apart from His Word?

7. Why does God want us to be active members of the church?

8. Why do you think God wants us to contribute cheerfully to the work of the church?

9. Why would we sit at the feet of great teachers?

10. Do you believe there is a connection between weak Bible knowledge and a weak passion for serving the Lord? Why or why not?

BIBLIOGRAPHY

Barnes, Albert. *Notes On The New Testament: Ephesians, Philippians, And Colossians.* Baker Book House, Grand Rapids, 1960.

Bell, Rob. *Velvet Elvis: Repainting The Christian Faith.* New York, New York: HarperCollins, 2012.

Book of Mormon, The. Salt Lake City, Utah: The Church of Jesus Christ of Latter-day Saints, 1981.

Chesser, Frank. *Thinking Right About God.* Huntsville, Alabama: Publishing Designs, 2014.

Chesterton, G.K. *The Common Man.* New York: Sneed & Ward, 1950.

Connor, Walter Thomas. *Revelation and God: An Introduction to Christian Doctrine.* Nashville, Tennessee: Broadman Press, 1936.

Cottrell, Jack. *The Faith Once For All: Bible Doctrine For Today.* Joplin, Missouri: College Press Publishing Company, 2004.

Doctrine and Covenants, The. Salt Lake City, Utah: The Church of Jesus Christ of Latter-day Saints, 1949.

Fischer, Austin. *Young, Restless, No Longer Reformed.* Eugene, Oregon: Cascade Books, 2014.

Geisler, Norman. *Systematic Theology: In One Volume.* Minneapolis, Minnesota: Bethany House, 2011.

Grudem, Wayne. *Bible Doctrine.* Grand Rapids, Michigan: Zondervan, 1999.

Helm, Paul. "Is God Bound by Time?" *God Under Fire.* Grand Rapids, Michigan: Zondervan, 2002.

Hippolytus. "The Refutation Of All Heresies, Book X, Chapter XXVIII. *The Ante-Nicene Fathers.* Volume 5. Peabody, Massachusetts: Hendrickson Publishers, 2012.

Jackson, Wayne. "Providence." *The Great I AM: Our Unsearchable God.* Henderson, Tennessee: Freed-Hardeman University, 1997.

Jackson, Wayne. "What About the Terms 'Godhead' and 'Trinity'?" www.ChristianCourier.com. Accessed 14 Mar 2016. < https://www.christiancourier.com/articles/821-what-about-the-terms-godhead-and-trinity >.

Lanier, Roy, Jr. "The Godhead." *What Do You Know About God? The Fourth Annual Missouri-Kansas Lectures,* ed. Jack H. Williams. Independence, Missouri: Williams Publishing, 1985.

Lanier, Roy, Sr. *The Timeless Trinity.* Denver, Colorado: Roy H. Lanier, Sr. Publishing, 1974.

Lewis, C.S. *Beyond The Personality: The Christian Idea of God.* New York, New York: The Macmillan Company, 1948.

Lewis, C.S. *God In The Dock.* Grand Rapids, Michigan: Eerdmans, 1970.

Lipscomb, David. *Queries And Answers.* Cincinnati, Ohio: F.L. Rowe, 1918.

Lucado, Max. *Grace For The Moment.* Nashville, TN: Thomas Nelson, 2000.

Mangina, Joseph L. *Karl Barth: Theologian of Christian Witness.* Louisville, Kentucky: Westminster John Knox Press, 2004.

May, Cecil, Jr. *Providence: The Silent Sovereignty of God.* Nashville, Tennessee: Gospel

Advocate Company, 2014.

McLaren, Brian, Tony Campolo. *Adventures In Missing The Point: How The Culture-Controlled Church Neutered The Gospel*. Grand Rapids, Michigan: Zondervan, 2003.

Miller, Dave. *Why People Suffer*. Montgomery, Alabama: Apologetics Press, 2015.

Morey, Robert A. *Death and the Afterlife*. Minneapolis, Minnesota: Bethany House, 1984.

Newport, Frank. "More Than 9 in 10 Americans Continue to Believe in God." *Gallup*. 3 June 2011. Accessed 9 Dec 2015. <http://www.gallup.com/poll/147887/Americans-Continue-Believe-God.aspx>.

Olson, Roger E. *Against Calvinism*. Grand Rapids, Michigan: Zondervan, 2011.

Packer, J.I. *Knowing God*. Downer's Grove, Illinois: InterVarsity Press, 1993.

Palmer, Edwin H. *The Five Points of Calvinism*. Grand Rapids, Michigan: Baker Publishing Group, 2006.

Pink, Arthur W. *The Attributes Of God*. Pensacola, Florida: Chapel Library, 1993.

Pink, Arthur W. *The Sovereignty Of God*. Grand Rapids, Michigan: Baker Book House, 1984.

Piper, John. "Confronting The Problem of Evil." *DesiringGod.org*. Accessed 17 Jan 2016. <http://www.desiringgod.org/articles/confronting-the-problem-s-of-evil>.

Piper, John. *The Pleasures of God*. Colorado Springs, Colorado: Multnomah Books, 2000.

Piper, John. "Why I Do Not Say, 'God Did Not Cause the Calamity, but He Can Use It for Good.'" 17 September 2001. *DesiringGod.org*. Accessed 25 January 2016. < http://www.desiringgod.org/articles/why-i-do-not-say-god-did-not-cause-the-calamity-but-he-can-use-it-for-good>.

Purkiser, W.T. *Exploring Our Christian Faith*. Kansas City, Missouri: Beacon Hill Press, 1978.

Scott, Thomas. *The Articles Of The Synod Of Dort*. Philadelphia: Presbyterian Board Of Publication, 1841.

Sire, James W. *The Universe Next Door: A Basic Worldview Catalog*. Downers Grove, Illinois: InterVarsity Press, 1997.

Smith, F. LaGard. *Troubling Questions for Calvinists*. Lynchburg, VA: Cotswald Publishing, 2007.

"Sovereign." *Merriam-Webster.com*. Merriam-Webster, 2015. Web. 21 Dec 2015.

Sproul, R. C. Jr. *Almighty Over All: Understanding The Sovereignty Of God*. Grand Rapids, Michigan: Baker Publishing Group, 1999.

Spurgeon, C. H. *The Autobiography of Charles H. Spurgeon, Compiled from His Letters, Diaries, and Records by His Wife and Private Secretary*. Vol. 4, Cincinnati, Ohio: Curtis & Jennings, 1900.

Spurgeon, Charles H. *The Treasury Of David*. Vol. 4. London: Marshall Brothers Ltd, 1882.

Spurgeon, Charles H. *The Treasury of David*. Vol. 5. New York, New York: Funk & Wagnalls, 1886.

Strong, A.H. *Systematic Theology*. Valley Forge, Pennsylvania: The Judson Press, 1963.

Tertullian. "Against Marcion." Book II, Chapter 5. *The Ante-Nicene Fathers*. Vol. 3. Peabody, Massachusetts: Hendrickson Publishers, 2012.

Thiessen, Henry Clarence. *Lectures In Systematic Theology.* Grand Rapids, Michigan, Eerdmans Publishing Company, 1989.

Thistlethwaite, Susan Brooks. "On the Trinity." *Interpretation.* Vol. 45, No. 2, 1991, p. 159.

Thompson, Bert. "Is God Male?" *ApologeticsPress.org.* Accessed 20 Mar 2016. < http://www.apologeticspress.org/APContent.aspx?category=11&article=1165>.

Thompson, John. *Modern Trinitarian Perspectives.* New York, New York: Oxford University Press, 1994.

Tozer, A.W. *The Knowledge of the Holy.* New York: Walker and Company, 1996.

Warburton, Ben A. *Calvinism.* Grand Rapids: Michigan: Erdman's Publishing Co., 1955

Warren, Thomas Bratton. "God and Evil: Does Judeo-Christian Theism Involve A Logical Contradiction?" *Doctoral Dissertation,* Vanderbilt University, 1969. University Microfilms, Inc., Ann Arbor, Michigan.

CPSIA information can be obtained
at www.ICGtesting.com
Printed in the USA
LVHW03s0733060818
585816LV00004B/11/P